# The Essence of Women in Management

Susan Vinnicombe and Nina L. Colwill

**Prentice Hall**

London   New York   Toronto   Sydney   Tokyo   Singapore
Madrid   Mexico City   Munich

First published 1995 by
Prentice Hall International (UK) Limited
Campus 400, Maylands Avenue
Hemel Hempstead
Hertfordshire, HP2 7EZ
A division of
Simon & Schuster International Group

Typeset in 10/12pt Palatino
by Keyset Composition, Colchester, Essex

Printed and bound in Great Britain by
T.J. Press (Padstow) Ltd, Padstow, Cornwall.

---

Library of Congress Cataloging-in-Publication Data

---

Vinnicombe, Susan.
    The essence of women in management / by Susan Vinnicombe
and Nina L. Colwill.
        p.   cm. — (The essence of management)
    Includes bibliographical references and index.
    ISBN 0-13-285370-1
    1. Women executives.    Colwill, Nina L. (Nina Lee)   II. Title.
III. Series
    HD6054.3.V56   1995
    331.4'816584—dc20

                                                                95-7759
                                                                CIP

---

British Library Cataloguing in Publication Data

---

A catalogue record for this book is available from
the British Library
ISBN 0-13-285370-1

---

1  2  3  4  5      99  98  97  96  95

# The Essence of Women in Management

*Dedicated to John and Dennis*

# Contents

vii

# Preface

> Organisations need talented women in their core jobs, therefore,
> not only for reasons of social fairness, important though that is,
> but because many of those women will have the kinds of attitudes
> and attributes that the new flat flexible organisations need. If they
> screen out the women they will handicap their futures.
>
> Charles Handy[1]

Why is there a need for such a book? Consider the following five
illustrations.

1. Britain's top woman surveyor, Mary Dent, went into the profession
   because she read on the back of a Quaker Oats packet, 'Why not let
   your daughter become a surveyor?'[2] She is Executive Director of
   Planning and Conservation with the Royal Borough of Kensington and
   Chelsea. In 1992 she was elected President of one of the divisions of
   the Royal Institute of Chartered Surveyors.

   Today women make up 17 per cent of the student membership of
   the Royal Institute of Chartered Surveyors but only 5.6 per cent of
   associates and fellows. Of student chartered accountants 37.1 per cent
   are women, but women form only 14.3 per cent of qualified members
   of the Institute of Chartered Accountants.[3]

2. Hilary Heilbron QC is one of only 41 women QCs of a total of 760 QCs.
   She is chairman of the Bar Council's Sex Discrimination Committee
   which produced a watershed report on sex discrimination at the Bar
   in 1992, commissioned by the Bar Council and the Lord Chancellor's
   Department. The report concluded that there is 'substantial evidence

of early and continuing unequal treatment between the sexes at many levels of the profession'.

Women now account for 20 per cent of independent barristers. In 1991, 42 per cent of those called to the Bar were women, yet at judicial level there are no Lords of Appeal in Ordinary, one woman Lord Justice of Appeal of 27, 3 women High Court Judges of 83 and only 19 women circuit judges of 421.

3. Alison Halford, who became the first woman Assistant Chief Constable after 20 years of service, abanadoned sex discrimination allegations against the Police Force and retired at 52. Her 40-day acrimonious court case was financially backed by the Equal Opportunities Commission, costing £1.2 million. Of the 86 posts of Chief Constable and Deputy Chief in England and Wales none is held by a woman.

4. Abigail Kirby-Harris, a former Army Captain, has filed a claim against the Army for £500,000 damages because she was dismissed from her Officer's post for becoming pregnant. The Ministry of Defence has already paid out £30 million in compensation to ex-servicewomen discharged while pregnant.

5. The Arthur Anderson Corporate Register, which surveyed all 20 000 public-company directors in Britain in 1994, found that despite a quarter of a century of equal opportunities, there were only 234 women directors, holding between them 113 executive directorships and 155 non-executive posts.[4]

The year I was born – 1948 – was the first year that women were permitted to attend Oxford University. But such progress – late in coming in the academic world as it was – has not been matched in the management world. Women were not allowed into the Stock Exchange, for example, until as late at the 1970s. 'Too rough, my friend', explained one pinstriped man, interviewed at the time, saying that there was too much shoving and pushing on the floor of the Stock Exchange and that the 'fair and fragile sex would be trampled underfoot'.

Kate Saunders, a journalist, writes about Opportunity 2000 three years after its fanfare launch by John Major in 1991:

When you begin to restore an ancient fresco caked with centuries of soot, the first little clear patch will have the effect of making the rest look dirtier. The optimistic third annual report from Opportunity 2000, the government-backed campaign for a more woman-friendly workforce, only highlights our pitiful lack of progress and the immensity of the task ahead.

Opportunity 2000 has 275 member companies in the public and private sectors, covering more than 25 per cent of the workforce.[5]

The obstacles to women taking their rightful places in the running of business and industry are still formidable and, some would argue, growing more intractable. The realignment of power needed to change the position of women in the working world is only gradually beginning to inch forward and may not make appreciable gains before the millennium.

Meanwhile, the male-dominated business world is denying itself the remarkable contributions women could make to wealth creation and the provision of services, and indeed are making, whenever opportunities for them to take visible roles in the management sphere are open to them. Part of this contribution is the sense of collaboration, cooperation, participation, empowerment, credit-sharing and involvement that women bring instinctively to their jobs. As the American feminist, Gloria Steinem, pointed out:

> Women tend to define power differently . . . traditional definitions of power have a lot to do with the ability to dominate other people and benefit unfairly from their work . . . We, as women, on the other hand, tend to define power as the ability to use our own talents and to control our own lives.[6]

If the radical re-engineering of companies continues to reshape them into small teams more responsive to customers, more sensitive to people and more in touch with their global markets, the need for women managers should grow exponentially. Already, management experts on both sides of the Atlantic are claiming that the management style of women better fits the demands of new organisations than their male counterparts.

Management guru Charles Handy puts it forcefully:

> For these jobs the organisations want quality people, well educated, well skilled and adaptable. They also want people who can juggle with several tasks and assignments at one time, who are more interested in making things happen than in what title or office they hold, more concerned with power and influence than status. They want people who value instinct and intuition as well as analysis and rationality, who can be tough but also tender, focused but friendly, people who can cope with these necessary contradictions. They want, therefore, as many women as they can get.[7]

Women in management is not a new topic, but it now has a new urgency; whereas in the past parallels were drawn between civil rights struggles and equal opportunities became the watchword for women everywhere with controversy around quotas and affirmative action. Today a clear business case can be made for increasing women's participation at all levels in the workforce. The business case for expanding the numbers and *elevating* the positions of women management is rooted in the context of managing employee diversity as a vital resource. Gender is one of six primary dimensions of diversity – those immutable human differences that are inborn and which exert powerful impact throughout a person's entire life. (The other primary dimensions of diversity are age, ethnicity, physical abilities/qualities or (disabilities) race and sexual/affectional orientation.)

The business case for increasing women in management therefore rests on three major supporting arguments:

1. Women's natural work style fits in better with the changes in jobs and the changing structure of organisations than their male counterparts' work style.

2. Women can give companies a competitive advantage in the global marketplace by helping them reflect better in their management teams the gender make-up of the markets into which they are selling.

3. Skilled women are a vital resource. As demographics result in a shortage of skilled employees in the run-up to the new millennium and beyond it will be imperative to recruit more women into management.

The business case for more women in management starts by looking at the predicted radical changes in work itself and those already taking place. Re-engineering, using self-managing teams, flattening hierarchies, designing computers to do routine work, using new technology to deliver complex information systems to frontline employees, thereby eliminating intermediaries, dejobbing or downsizing will make many jobs redundant.

The focus will shift from structured jobs to the work that needs to be done, from traditional job holders to competent people who are flexible in their approach to work, not worried about status and the trappings of status, entrepreneurial, empowering, flexible, multi-tasking, capable of working in self-managing teams, employee-nurturers, and good verbal communicators. These traits and qualities favour women managers and their preferred natural ways of working. This close fit between women and the changing nature of work and managerial style should, of itself, increase a company's desire to hire and to retain and promote qualified women managers.

There are human resources issues favouring the recruitment of more women managers. As career ladders disappear, managers will be expected to have portable career portfolios and the emphasis will shift from career development in one company to personal development in many.

Since personal development and intrinsic work satisfaction motivates women more than traditional career development up the hierarchy, with its associated package of salary, status and company perks, women are again better suited to embrace the kinds of careers on offer in organisations.

Women have always needed to take a more holistic approach to life, balancing work with family needs. As the structure and attitudes of society change towards management, more single parent families and women with elderly relatives will be at an advantage in dealing with these future changes.

*Management in the Millennium*, a report by Britain's top firms, looked into the skills needed in the next century. These skills naturally favour women – and include interpersonal skills, change management, communication skills, the ability to listen and to relate to others. Ten years ago there were only a dozen women branch managers at Abbey National. Today there are 315 women branch managers, half the total number. Jane Ageros, Head of Corporate Affairs at Abbey National plc, says that many of these women bank managers will move up into more senior positions and that the trend is 'unstoppable'.

In a BBC *Panorama* programme 'The Future is Female'[8] Professor Dennis Malfese of the University of Southern Illinois said: 'If our future society tends to continue to develop the way it is, in terms of becoming more complex [requiring] information managers, relying on verbal skills, the creation of documents, the assimilation of information, one would suspect that's going to advantage females a great deal.'

In the UK one million new jobs, mainly part-time jobs for women, will be created between now and the year 2000, according to the Institute for Employment Research of Warwick University. This increase, the Institute predicts, will come from cyclical recovery rather than long-term growth. Unfortunately this spurt in employment growth will be offset by a continuing decline of male full-time employment and unemployment will remain above the 2 million mark until the end of the century. On the positive side the Institute's predictions include a growth in industrial output of 3.3 per cent per year from 1993–7 and an increase in individual productivity by 2.7 per cent – the best performance for 40 years.

By 2010 Caucasian males will account for less than 40 per cent of the total American labour force, according to the research report of the Hudson Institute.[9] Of the more than 20 million jobs that are expected to be created in the United States in the run-up to the new millennium, women and people of colour are expected to fill 75 per cent of them. Diversity in gender, age, ethnic heritage, physical ability, race and sexual/affectional orientation are increasing in the workplace as US society becomes more culturally diverse. In Europe in general by 2025 more than 20 per cent of the population will be over 65 years old. Eighty per cent of the new entrants to the labour market could soon be women.

There is a marketing advantage that comes from increasing women and the other minorities in the workforce. As the EU draws its member states into ever-closer union, as barriers between countries collapse and mobility of labour increases and as markets become increasingly global, there are strong strategic and marketing reasons for having a diverse senior management team that reflects the pluralistic and global markets into which a company is selling. If the marketplace continues to become more and more multicultural and if the purchasing power of women continues to rise, there are advantages to reflecting this rainbow perspective within a company's own management.

As Rosabeth Moss Kanter observed:

> Today both women and men have a stake in equal opportunity issues. Full development of human resources is a key competitive advantage in the knowledge society. Meritocracy – letting talent rise to the top regardless of where it is found and whether it is male or female – is essential to business success in free-market economies. Within this context, the quality of women in the work force is no longer a politically correct luxury. It has become a competitive necessity.[10]

Demographics indicate a scarcity of skilled workers in the first decade of the next century. Recognising this, companies are framing policies and developing implementation strategies on managing employee diversity as a vital resource. The argument is a simple one – as skilled diverse employees (women, racial minorities and others) recognise their value as scarce resources, they will look to companies with proven track records (not simply hastily drafted policies) of managing women and diverse employees before accepting positions. Those companies whose boards and senior management teams mirror a real commitment to women and to other diverse employees will have a competitive advantage in recruiting the skills and mix of management needed to thrive.

Beyond the business case for increasing women in management there still remain the strong philosphical, ethical, social and political arguments of ending discrimination of all types in the workplace. The arguments supporting women's role in management converge from all directions. It has not been easy, in writing this book, to examine each argument discretely. Perhaps it is not even necessary to do so since all that rises must converge.

*The Essence of Women in Management*, then, examines the rationale for expanding opportunities for women to achieve a more equal representation in management positions. It explores research on the status of women managers in Europe, analyses female roles in organisations, looks at the balancing act between work and family, examines the plethora of research on sex differences and illuminates the underlying issue of power and powerlessness. The book puts forward strategies for shattering the artificial glass ceilings to women's advancement to senior management posts. These strategies include women-only training, networking, mentoring protégés, assessment and the Government's intervention for women managers: Opportunity 2000.

Of course, many of the underlying issues here have a long history. Jane Austen (1775–1817) complained about the inequalities between men and women of her own day. 'Yes, yes, if you please, no reference to examples in books', she wrote. 'Men have had every advantage of us telling their own story. Education has been theirs in so much higher a degree; the pen has been in their hands, I will not allow books to prove anything.'

We offer this slender volume to you, dear reader, to help redress the balance.

SUSAN VINNICOMBE

# References

1. Handy, Charles, *The Empty Raincoat*, Hutchinson, London, 1994.
2. *The Times*, 30 June 1992.
3. Clement, Barrie, 'Women in professions "Fighting a Sex War"', *Independent*, 14 November 1994.
4. Lynn, Matthew, 'Old boys top of the business class', *Sunday Times*, 6 November 1994.
5. Saunders, Kate, 'High anxiety in the real world of work', *Sunday Times*, 6 November 1994.
6. Steinem, Gloria, *Outrageous Acts and Everyday Rebellions*, Jonathan Cape, London, 1984, p. 200 *et seq.*
7. Handy, Charles, op. cit., p. 179.
8. BBC *Panorama*, 'The future is female', 24 October 1994.
9. Johnson, William B. and Packer, Arnold H., *Workforce 2000*, Hudson Institute, Indianapolis, 1987.
10. Nichols, Nancy A., *Reach for the Top* (foreword by Rosabeth Moss Kanter), Harvard Business Review Publications, Boston, 1994, p. ix.

# Acknowledgements

Victor Hugo's words 'Nothing can withstand the force of an idea whose time has come' are true and apply aptly to the theme of this book of increasing numbers of women in management; but while the idea creates its own momentum and is invincible, it is extremely useful to have help with such an idea.

The help we have had has come from many quarters – from our students, from colleagues, from our Universities and from the women managers with whom we have worked in many different countries. They have all contributed to our understanding of the complex issues facing women managers.

Particular thanks go to Joan Edwards who typed most of this book from early drafts to finished manuscript. Tammy Wright took responsibility for the chapters written in Canada and receives our gratitude. Erla Colwill Anderson produced the index for the book and deserves our thanks. Lastly, this book would never have reached conclusion without the constant chasing, encouraging, coaching and monitoring of John Bank, whose help was greatly appreciated.

Susan Vinnicombe,
London, England

Nina L. Colwill,
Brandon, Manitoba, Canada

# 1

# European Women in Management

## Susan Vinnicombe and Jane Sturges

Rather than just responding to the Economic Community's policies, women need to be at the centre of the debate about the single market and its effect on women. The women's movement will increasingly have to look at campaigns to extend women's rights with a European and international focus.

Jane Pillinger[1]

Forty per cent of the European workforce is female, according to statistics compiled by the European Community. Yet women's entry *en masse* into the workplace has by no means guaranteed them access to top jobs on a similar scale. With accurate figures hard to come by, an optimistic estimate suggests that just 10 per cent of European managers are female. When one considers senior management positions, the figure is far smaller.

The influx of women into the European workforce has been one of the dominant social trends during the past 30 years: women are entirely responsible for the growth in employment in the EU since the 1960s. Between 1965 and 1991, the number of women employed within the European Community rose from just under 40 million to just over 53 million. During the same period, the number of men employed fell slightly from 83 million to 82 million.[2]

In particular, the activity rate of women of prime working (and child-rearing) age, that is aged 25 to 49 years, has risen dramatically. In some countries, such as Denmark, Finland and France, most women continue in employment after they have children and in others, such as Germany and the UK, women's working careers are also showing less signs of interruption. By the end of the century in many European

1

countries, half the workforce will be female, although there are still significant differences in the number of women employed in the various EU member states.[3]

Countries where the number of women in the labour force is above average, that is more than 40 per cent of those employed, include the United Kingdom, Denmark, France and Portugal. Those where women account for a much lower proportion of the workforce (between 34 per cent and 37 per cent) in general are those whose national cultures reflect the strong influence of the Catholic Church and its attitude to the family, especially in southern Europe. They include Italy, Spain, Greece, Ireland and Luxembourg.

EU figures for women's participation in the workforce are likely to be lower than those for Western Europe as a whole, as they do not include Scandinavian countries such as Sweden and Finland, where the numbers of employed women virtually equal the numbers of employed men.[4]

According to the European Community Labour Force Survey, women's share of the workforce increased almost continuously in all EC member states between 1983 and 1991, with those countries with the lowest shares tending to experience the highest rates of increase.

Such statistics are deceptive, however; barriers to women in the workplace have not disappeared in Europe, for most women are still employed at a relatively menial level and many work part time. While the proportion of women in the workforce has increased, this increase has not been either in traditionally male-dominated industries, such as engineering, construction and transport or in traditionally male-dominated jobs, such as management.

The growth in women's jobs in Europe has occurred in a few sectors of employment and in a small number of jobs seen as being traditionally feminine. The sectors where jobs have been created over the past 10 years have tended to be those where women were already an important part of the labour force. The biggest increase in the number of women employed within the EU has been in clerical and service jobs, and while there has been a significant proportion of women with good educational qualifications moving into more senior positions, these jobs remain concentrated in public sector work such as teaching. In 1991 more than 75 per cent of women in work were employed in service industries, compared with only 20 per cent in the manufacturing industry.[2] Within service industries, the largest concentration of women's jobs are in what the EU classifies as 'other services' such as health and education or the distribution and catering sector. Fifty-five per cent of women worked in these two sectors in 1991, compared with 52 per cent in 1983. Within industry, women's jobs are concentrated in textiles, clothing and other labour-intensive industries.

# Part-time work

A significant number of women within the EU workforce work part time (28%, compared with just 4% of men). Clearly, this is partly a response to the problems of combining work with child-care and family responsibilities, which will be discussed in more detail below, but also underlines the menial nature of most women's work, in that it is undertaken as a job rather than a career. Part-time work is a career killer. It is generally only part-time work that is available at the lower levels of the organisation, where it offers no opportunities of advancement. There is less security attached to part-time jobs than to full-time jobs, although much research has demonstrated how committed many part-time workers are to their jobs. Part-time jobs are also much more economical to management, as they usually command relatively low salaries and restricted employee benefits, such as pensions.

Most employers who allow or even encourage part-time work or job-sharing for lower-grade employees often refuse to extend such schemes to management jobs. The recession seems to have emphasised this reluctance to make managers part time. 'With lots of competitive pressures we're giving managers more employees to manage. It wouldn't be fair on employees, nor on managers, to expect them to manage 10 or 20 employees part-time', says IBM Manager, Alan Drinkwater.[5] This organisational resistance against part-time managerial jobs runs counter to a number of current organisational trends. If dejobbing and boundaryless careers take off then the full-time senior manager will be a thing of the past.

# Women in management

Women occupy only about 10 per cent of management positions in Europe. Furthermore, women managers remain concentrated in junior and middle management positions: very few have managed to break through the 'glass ceiling' to occupy the top jobs.

It is difficult to put a more accurate figure on the numbers of women in management in Europe, first because different countries may have a different definition of a 'manager', and secondly because in many countries there are no regularised systems of gathering statistics in this area. Davidson and Cooper[6] (1993) estimate that women occupy fewer than 5 per cent of senior management roles, and suggest that this figure may be as high as 8 per cent in Greece and as low as 2 per cent in the United Kingdom. However, they estimate that, when all levels of management are considered, the United Kingdom has the highest number of women 'managers' at 26 per cent, compared with France at 25 per cent and Ireland at 17.4 per cent.

Even so, British industry is an overwhelmingly male bastion, dominated by middle-aged men who play golf and who have been to public school and Oxbridge.[7] Over the past two years, the number of women managers actually fell. The recession has pushed the equal opportunities timetable off the industrial agenda temporarily in those businesses struggling to survive. In the 1980s women were going to fill the gap left by the demographic time bomb, by an anticipated drop of 25 per cent in the number of 18-year-olds and by skill shortages. The single European market also helped to create job opportunities for women. This situation has now altered, for the moment. With unemployment at around 3 million, the skill shortages issue is no longer the issue it once was, but it is still a concern even if the skill shortages are more segmented. For example, the banking industry, which has been a major employer of women, is down-sizing and therefore not experiencing a skill shortage at present. However, it would be a mistake to think that the demographic bomb has been defused. Instead of focusing on solving skill shortages, women are providing the flexibility and new management styles needed in business in the 1990s to enhance performance.

Figures gathered by Antal and Krebsbach-Gnath[8] suggest that in the former West Germany 23.3 per cent of public sector managers are female, compared with only 5.9 per cent of private sector managers. Germany shows a high degree of job segregation by sex. In the former West Germany, for example, 70 per cent of women are concentrated in 10 occupational categories: women account for 86 per cent of people employed in the health services, 79 per cent in the social services, 62 per cent in retailing and 48 per cent in teaching. Not surprisingly, in Germany women tend to have a better chance of obtaining a management position in these sectors of the economy.

In France, the number of women employed in *cadre* (managerial) occupations appears higher than elsewhere in Europe, but this may be a function of definition rather than any real achievement. According to the French statistical institute, INSEE, by 1989 women accounted for 25 per cent of administrative and commercial managers but only 9.8 per cent of engineers and technical managers. Claims[9] that, although women have made progress in management, this progress has been limited to middle management, suggests that they have not yet reached chief executive or senior executive positions in French organisations. For example, only 10 per cent of top grade civil servants are female.

In France, as elsewhere in Europe, women's work remains highly segregated. Occupations such as low-skilled administrative positions, social and health work and primary school teaching are still largely female professions. Nevertheless, with nursery school placement available to all children over 3 years, child-care facilities are better in France than they are elsewhere. That may explain why part-time employment is less common there than in other countries.

One would assume that female managers would have the greatest chance of achieving success in the Scandinavian countries, where some of the highest numbers of women in the workforce are recorded, and family policies and equal opportunities programmes are strongly enforced by legislation. Yet the numbers of women managers do not appear to be significantly higher in Scandinavian countries than they are elsewhere in Europe. In Denmark, it is estimated that around 10 per cent of women in both the private and public sectors hold middle management jobs. A 1991 survey showed that only 4 per cent of 755 company directors were women.[10] In Finland the figures appear to be somewhat higher: Hanninen-Salmelin and Petajaniemi[4] claim that in 1990, 21 per cent of 'senior officials and executives' were women. Still, even here women managers are concentrated in areas such as banking and the public sector: they continue to be poorly represented in most private organisations.

In southern Europe the situation for women managers is more complex. While women have traditionally been less career-orientated in many southern Europe countries, there are now signs that there is strong growth in the numbers of women in the workforce and the numbers of women managers. In Italy and Spain younger women in particular appear to have a different attitude to work and are embarking upon management careers. Their numbers, however, remain low: in Italy, women occupy 3 per cent of upper management positions; in Spain, 5 per cent of private sector management jobs are filled by women.[6] As elsewhere in Europe, women managers in the south tend to be concentrated in jobs in the service and public sectors.

# Equal pay

Just as their entry into the workforce has not assured European women of access to top jobs, so it also has not guaranteed them equal pay. In the United Kingdom, for example, women earn around 75 per cent of men's gross weekly earnings.[11] This situation is repeated throughout the EU. Male manual workers in manufacturing industry earn approximately 25 per cent more per hour than women. In Denmark and Italy the gap appears to be closing faster than elsewhere: women there are paid 85 per cent of the men's rate.[6]

The position for the few women who have managed to break into management is no better: they are still paid less than their male colleagues.

In some countries the gap between average male and female earnings is larger than it is for manual workers; in others it is smaller. For example, in the United Kingdom the highest paid women earn approximately 30 per cent less than the highest paid men. The gap between male and female managers is similar to this in France.[12] In the Netherlands, it is as high as 40 per cent. In Germany, on the other hand, while women earn about one-third less than men do overall, the earnings gap between male and female managers is smaller, with women being paid approximately 20 per cent less than their male colleagues.[8]

## Qualifications and age

This discrepancy cannot be justified on the grounds of lack of qualifications. The evidence is that throughout Europe women are now as well, if not better, educated than their male counterparts. In the United Kingdom, around three-fifths of further education students are now female, double the number of 21 years ago.[11] In a provocative BBC *Panorama* documentary television programme entitled 'The Future is Female',[13] the BBC exploded the myth that males catch up in education as they develop physically both in GCSEs and A levels. Females have opened up a commanding and increasing lead over their male counterparts in all subject areas *except* science and maths where they are even in results. In France 46 per cent of girls and 36 per cent of boys pass the baccalaureate, and over half the university students are female.[12] In Italy, women constitute 50 per cent of those studying at university. It seems that beliefs rather than qualifications discriminate against women. Men are convinced that they are more intelligent than women, even rating their fathers as brighter than their mothers, according to Halla Beloff's research.[14] So strong are these cultural beliefs that women students also underestimate their own intelligence and believe that their fathers are more clever than their mothers. Such beliefs damage women's professional prospects by lowering women's self confidence.

Women still appear to lag behind their male counterparts when it comes to studying for business qualifications in most countries: while France claims that 50 per cent of its business school students are female,[14] in Italy 26 per cent of those obtaining graduate degrees from management and business schools are women.[15] In the United Kingdom, the Association of MBAs estimates that the proportion of women MBA graduates now stands at around 25 per cent – much lower than the North American figure.

There is little evidence about whether female managers tend to be older or younger than their male counterparts, and that which does exist is conflicting. Davidson and Cooper found in 1984 that UK women managers were slightly older than men.[6] This may be a function of the greater difficulty they have in reaching top jobs and the longer time that it takes them to do so. In southern Europe, on the other hand, it appears that women managers are young, possibly because the social changes which have allowed them to undertake careers took place more recently there than they did in some northern European countries. In Italy, for example, research by the University of Bocconi's Centre for Research on Company Organisation[16] into senior women managers found that almost half of them were under 45 years.

## Marriage and children

What is certain is that women managers throughout Europe are far more likely to be single and/or childless than their male colleagues. Combining work with child-rearing continues to be stressful for most women and it is clear that some organisations have compounded this problem by operating a double standard for marriage: they view the married male manager as an asset, with a stable support network at home allowing him to give his undivided attention to his work, but the married female manager as a liability, likely to neglect her career at the expense of her family at every possible opportunity. 'Professional women today are being caught between a rock and a hard place', says Professor Ethel Roskies. 'On the one hand, they're told, "If you want to get ahead for success, you better not get married and have kids." On the other hand, the stereotype of the old maid is still with us – you can only be happy if you're married and have kids.'[17]

It is not surprising, therefore, that many women managers have had little choice but to take this double standard for marriage into account in their career strategies, avoiding the responsibility of family commitments wherever possible. Research carried out in the United Kingdom by the British Institute of Management showed that only 58 per cent of women managers are married, compared with 93 per cent of male managers. Of the married women, half have children compared with nearly nine out of ten of their married male counterparts. In other words, male managers are three times more likely to have children than their female colleagues. Other research[18] showed that married women were highly likely to have spouses in full-time employment, whereas men surveyed were in a similar position. If organisations want to attract more women into management then there needs to be a fundamental change of attitude, one that adapts to the reality of women's lives.

The situation appears to be much the same for women managers elsewhere in Europe. In the former West Germany only 40 per cent of women managers are mothers, and they usually have only one child. In contrast, almost all their male colleagues are married and have an average of two children.[8] In a survey carried out in a large computer company in France,[12] the women managers were more likely to be unmarried and not to have children. Of those who did have children, the vast majority had only one or two. There is some evidence that this situation may be changing: in Italy research by CRORA showed that women were more likely to be married now than they were a decade ago.[16]

It is agreed that a key problem faced by women pursuing a career is finding a supportive partner, not only one who is prepared to share family and household responsibilities but who will not feel threatened by a woman earning more and being more successful than they. Anita Roddick of the Body Shop, millionaire and mother, has gone on record as saying 'Of course you can have it all – it's all down to the partner you choose. We need better editing of partners in life.'[19] Research has shown that women managers are much more likely to be divorced or separated than men; even in Catholic countries divorce rates for women managers appear to be on the increase: according to CRORA's[16] research the Italian women managers they surveyed were twice as likely to be divorced or separated in 1987 than they were in 1975.

While it has now become the norm for many educated men to espouse a belief in sharing household duties with their partners, their behaviour falls short of the belief. In the United Kingdom, 73 per cent of women still do 'nearly all the housework' and that men with working partners have an average of six hours more spare time at weekends than their partners do.[20] While child-care responsibility tends to be more evenly shared, men are likely to be involved in the more pleasurable aspects of it; for example, taking the children to the cinema or theatre. In the Netherlands, women spend 15 per cent of every working day on housework, whereas men only spend 4 per cent.[21] In France, employed mothers devote 48 of every 100 hours to domestic work and 52 to professional activities, while men devote 28 to domestic work and 72 to professional activities.[9]

As can be seen in Chapter 3, the main responsibility for household tasks still lies with women throughout Europe. This poses a particular problem for women managers, in that managerial jobs have traditionally been structured to suit a man who has a wife at home providing him with a full-time support system. Even if women managers do not have children, they still have to contend with other family responsibilities which many of their male colleagues do not share. Women managers who do wish to combine a career with raising a family must deal with maternity benefits and the provision of child care which are difficult to acquire. Some writers believe that child-care facilities are the key block to women achieving managerial jobs in the United Kingdom.

# Parental benefits

With regard to parental benefits, the Scandinavian countries have traditionally led Europe. In Finland, for example, families are entitled to a total
of 281 days' parental leave, while being paid 80 per cent of their salary.[4]
Most of this benefit can be shared between the mother and the father, as
the parents wish. (It is interesting to note that while parental leave is
available to all men, they do not necessarily take advantage of it. In 1990
only 40 per cent of Finnish fathers took paternity leave on the birth of a
child; only 3 per cent used the full 170 days available to them, and these
men tended to be younger and better educated that average.) In Sweden
parents are entitled to 15 months of leave, 12 of which will be paid at
statutory benefit rates which equal 90 per cent of average earnings.[22] As
of May 1994 fathers have to take at least three months of this leave.

Other countries, such as Germany, the Netherlands and Portugal, now
offer full maternity leave pay, albeit in all cases for a relatively short period
of time. In Germany mothers receive 14 weeks paid maternity leave: after
this period, either parent can take an 18-month leave, during which period
they are entitled to a state-paid allowance, calculated according to the
recipient's income.[8] Ninety-seven per cent of those eligible take the leave,
but in almost 99 per cent of cases it is the mother, and not the father, who
does so. (Of the fathers who have taken leave, 70 per cent were
unemployed prior to doing so.) There are now plans to extend the leave
to two and eventually three years.[8]

In the Netherlands women receive 16 weeks' maternity leave; in addition
it is possible for women and men to reduce working hours to a minimum
of 20 hours per week for 6 months when they have children under 4
years.[21] In France mothers are paid 90 per cent of their salary for a period
of between 16 and 18 weeks,[12] after which many are allowed to take
between 1 and 3 years unpaid leave.

The pattern of allowing mothers to take a period of maternity leave of
a few months when they are paid most of their salary, combined with a
longer unpaid period, is now becoming the norm throughout Europe. The
terms of the Social Protocol, signed by 11 members of the EC (excluding
the United Kingdom) in 1992, establish a minimum of 14 weeks' maternity
pay to all employed women in the Community without any qualifying
conditions.

The United Kingdom has the poorest statutory maternity provisions in
Europe. The legislation has so many exclusion clauses that half of all
employed women in the United Kingdom receive no maternity leave at
all.[23] While the United Kingdom allows the longest period of time off work
to those who are entitled to it (40 weeks) in Europe, most British women
receive only half their salary during the period they are away from work.

Some companies compensate for this low level of statutory benefits by offering their own, more generous maternity packages. (One in four UK employers enhance statutory maternity leave, compared with only a sixth of Swedish employers.) Nevertheless, only 10 per cent of women in the United Kingdom enjoy extended maternity leave arrangements.

In some organisations in the United Kingdom not only are there poor maternity leave arrangements but worse still, maternity becomes an excuse for dismissal. The Ministry of Defence was compelled to pay out over £30 million in compensation to ex-servicewomen discharged while pregnant. The Equal Opportunities Commission reports that pregnancy dismissal is commonplace. Paula Wilkes, head of the Commission's family unit, said: 'According to our research 4,000 pregnant women lose their jobs every year; and that is despite new legislation aimed to strengthen the maternity rights of employed women.'

In July 1994 the European Court of Justice ruled that employers who dismiss women for becoming pregnant will automatically be guilty of sex discrimination. These employers will also face the possibility of unlimited claims for compensation as the new legislation has swept away a low ceiling on damages. In October 1994 a European Union directive gave *all* employed women the right to a minimum of 14 weeks' maternity leave, eliminating the former requirement of 2 years' employment to qualify.

There is a common practice of either eliminating the pregnant woman's job or radically restructuring it to make it incompatible with her new family obligations. This was the case for Susan Caro, a former film editor at ITN: when the new terms and conditions were created around her old job, she chose voluntary redundancy. 'I already had one small child and I was pregnant with my second', she said; 'the new working practices would have required me to do unlimited overtime, with no ceiling on it, whenever it was required, and I knew that it would be impossible to look after one child, let alone two.' The restructured job did offer more money, but that was not her point. She believes that the male managers who changed her job with the new contract wanted to shake her out. 'I think they thought that by having children I'd let down the very macho, hard-drinking world of news and current affairs', she said. 'They expect you to prop up the bar for hours after the programme has gone out, and if you have a life outside of your job the men don't really like it.'[24]

## Child-care

Child-care poses even more complicated problems for women managers who decide to return to work after a period of maternity leave. Public facilities for the care of under-3s, in particular, are not available in many countries and large numbers of parents have to make their own, often expensive, arrangements unless they work for an organisation which has its own in-house day-care centre. There are wide variations in government-controlled child-care facilities throughout Europe, although once again the Scandinavian countries offer a better provision than other parts of Europe. Finland provides child-care services for all children from the age of 1 year: municipal day-care centres are open from 7 a.m. to 6 p.m. and provide meals for the children.[4] In Denmark almost half of children up to the age of 2 years are looked after in crêches.[25]

France and Belgium both offer nursery education for all children from the age of 3 years, with some crêches available for children under this age. The situation in the former West Germany is somewhat worse: there are crêche places for only 2 per cent of babies and nursery places for just under 80 per cent of 3–6 year-olds.[8] Once again, the United Kingdom lags far behind many of its northern European neighbours. It is estimated that only 1.3 per cent of under-5s in the United Kingdom have a nursery place. In the 20 years from 1962, the number of places in local government day nurseries only grew from 22 000 to 30 000. The number of places in private nurseries has grown far more rapidly but this is an expensive option and child-care expenses are not tax-deductible in the United Kingdom.

## Equal opportunities and legislation

Sexual harassment plagues employed women and many countries lack the legal means to combat it. The International Labour Organisation highlighted that only 7 of the 23 countries surveyed – Australia, Canada, France, New Zealand, Spain, Sweden and the United States – have statutes that refer to or define sexual harassment; 6 to 8 per cent of employed women change jobs due to sexual harassment and a further 15–30 per cent have experienced serious problems such as unwanted touching and offensive sexual commentary. The figures vary across Europe – 21 per cent of French women, 58 per cent of Dutch women and an alarming 74 per cent of British women have reported being sexually harassed at work. Even these figures may distort the facts, since as many as 60 per cent of harassment cases go unreported. 'Sexual harassment is one of the most offensive and demeaning experiences an employee can suffer', says Michael Rubinstein, a consultant on sexual harassment to the European Community.[26]

Paradoxically, despite the difficulty European women managers face in reaching senior positions, the issue of equal opportunities has a long history and a high profile. The principle of non-discrimination in employment between men and women dates back to the late 1950s, when it was incorporated into the founding treaty of the European Community in 1957. EU legislation has, however, tended to be based on the concept of ensuring equal treatment, rather than on creating equality by remedying past discrimination.[22]

Some national legislation has attempted to oblige employers to introduce equality measures. Under French legislation of 1983, employers have to produce annual equality audits, which detail distribution of recruitment, training, promotion, wage and job categories by sex. If there is an imbalance between male and female employees, measures to achieve greater equality must be introduced. In reality, most employers have ignored this legislation with impunity.[22]

Since 1991 Italy has had regional equality offices with powers to demand similar action from employers. For more than 20 years, Swedish organisations have had to show what measures they are taking to improve equality between men and women. In the United Kingdom equal opportunities policies at organisational level are guided by a statutory Code of Practice and the powers of the Equal Opportunities Commission.

Equal pay and equal opportunities legislation is now in place in all Western European countries, yet its effect on the jobs that women do and their position in organisational hierarchies has so far been minimal. While the number of women managers in Europe has increased over the past 10 years, it is still very small.

For this reason, in most countries there are now initiatives, both at national and at organisational level, which extend beyond equal opportunities legislation to try to raise the numbers of women in such traditionally male-dominated occupations as management.

Pressure for change has intensified in the light of social and demographic trends which are seeing the gradual breakdown of the nuclear family in many parts of Europe, with divorce, cohabitation and remarriage on the increase, and a fall in the birthrate to well below an average of two children in most countries, giving most women the opportunity of a life of virtually continuous employment, if they wish.

## Initiatives to increase the number of women managers

In many European countries there have been initiatives to try to increase the number of women managers working in the public sector, so that the government itself is seen to set a good example. In the late 1980s Denmark launched an equal opportunities action plan within its government departments, one aim of which was to raise women's share of management positions. A small increase from 9 per cent to 11 per cent was recorded between 1989 and 1990.[25] A similar programme has also been in operation in Germany.

In those countries where there have been attempts to influence private sector employers it has invariably been on a voluntary basis. Companies trying to promote equal opportunities and, in particular, the cause of women managers therefore still remain in a minority. The Price Water-house Cranfield project researchers estimated that in 1991 the number of organisations monitoring women's progress in terms of promotions ranged from 39 per cent in Spain to just 11 per cent in Denmark.[27]

'Family-friendly' employment policies offering flexible working arrangements are more popular, particularly in Scandinavia and Germany, where three-quarters of companies claim they offer them. The figure is lower in the United Kingdom and France where it is estimated that 40 per cent of organisations provide them. However, it is difficult to judge what effect such policies may have on the number of women managers since in many countries, such as the United Kingdom, part-time working is not seen as an option for senior staff. (A larger share of part-time workers in the Netherlands and Germany are said to be in professional jobs.[22])

In France only about 35 firms, including Moulinex, IBM and Roussel Uclaf, have implemented positive action schemes, generally after negotiating a *plan d'égalité* with their trade unions.[9] Such schemes generally include the issues of recruitment and access to positions with the company, training and career development. Belgium has also taken a voluntary approach to affirmative action, following a Royal decree passed in 1987 recommending that private enterprises actively pursue equality of opportunity for men and women.[28] Only 40 companies joined the government-sponsored pilot programme.

Portugal has adopted a raft of positive action measures through its Institute for Employment and Professional Training. The measures include the exemption of employers from 25 per cent or 50 per cent contribution to training grants when they employ women in traditionally male-dominated professions and a job creation grant, payable to companies for each new job they create for women in male-dominated professions.

# Opportunity 2000

In the United Kingdom there has been a recent history of equal opportunity initiatives in some larger organisations, in particular in the banking sector where employers are dependent on potential women managers as an important resource.

Since 1990, however, the main programme aimed at improving the position of women in British companies has been Opportunity 2000, the first national initiative of this kind in the United Kingdom. The initiative was developed by a group of 17 chairmen, chief executives and directors (11 men and 6 women) of major UK companies, working as a target team for the Business in the Community venture, a charity working on social and economic issues under the patronage of the Prince of Wales.

While Opportunity 2000 is not only government-funded, it is supported by the government and was officially launched by Prime Minister John Major in October 1991. The 17 founder members had grown to a group of 220 by the end of 1992,[29] including government departments, retailers such as Kingfisher and Sainsbury, privatised utilities such as BT and British Gas, and a range of other organisations from ICI to Legal & General.

While membership is voluntary, members must pay a fee related to the number of people employed. All members must make three commitments: to set their own goals for increasing opportunities for women in the workforce by the year 2000; to publish these goals; and to monitor and report on progress regularly. Although setting quotas for numbers of women is illegal in the United Kingdom, the concept of goals has apparently proved acceptable.

One of the target team's first actions was to commission research to find out why equal opportunities legislation and policies were having such a limited effect on women's position at work. It concluded that changing policies and procedures on their own was not enough, and that only a shift in organisational cultures would bring women fully into the mainstream of organisational life. Opportunity 2000's approach is therefore based on a model of cultural change, around four key elements: demonstrating commitment; changing behaviour; building ownership; and making the investment. (The initiative has also stressed the business case for equal opportunity, in particular the benefits it can offer organisations in terms of improving their customer orientation.)

Many organisations participating in Opportunity 2000 are closely monitoring the effects of their actions on women managers, but as yet it is too soon to determine the long-term effects of the initiative. It still remains to be seen, therefore, whether such a voluntary approach to improving the lot of women in the workforce can succeed. However, the number of companies participating have already given Opportunity 2000 a higher profile and greater muscle than any other European initiative to date.

## Eastern European women in management

Five years after the fall of the Berlin Wall and three years after the end of the Soviet Union, private enterprise thrives across Eastern Europe. The surprise collapse of communism that came with spectacular speed in 1989 and the dramatic rebuilding of the economies of Eastern European countries, together with the redefinition of the former Soviet Union's role have created a special situation for Eastern European women in management. Women in two dozen countries need to sort through the wreckage of a half century of central planning to find their rights and new opportunities.

Preparations to open the European Union to Eastern Europe, begun in late 1994, should make substantial progress by the summer of 1995 when a White Paper will reveal what will be required of each of the ex-communist countries to apply to join the European Union. Two areas where Eastern European states will have particular difficulties in adopting EU legislation are the social chapter and the environment. Women in employment and management will be part of the social chapter considerations and a key element in a wider debate.

The legacy of the past had its special problems. Under the communist systems established after World War II, women were a resource to be used if needed like any other resource of the planned economies. In Poland, for example, the number of women in the workforce fluctuated depending on the level of political tension, the need for women workers to advance state plans to modernise the economy and the shortage of available male workers. There were also ideological arguments for women's opportunities based on equality. The Polish United Workers Party (PUWP), one of the most powerful components of the Communist Party, for example, declared at a national congress in the 1970s that: 'Women should be more often selected to managerial and supervisory posts provided their personal traits, professional knowledge, and moral standards can guarantee their responsible work in leadership positions.'

As Renata Siemienska, an expert on the topic, observed:

The increase in the number of University-educated women in the labour force had a moderate effect on the number of women in higher managerial positions after World War II. Thus, women's under-representation in higher positions in some sectors has been due not to a lack of qualified women, but rather to decisions made by the Communist government concerning when and how many women they would hire at any given time. In addition, compared to men, women were appointed or elected to positions that gave them less control over the distribution of resources.[30]

Today in Poland's post-Communist rebuilding, even fewer women are being elected to parliament than in the Communist period when a quota system prevailed. But more women are finding managerial jobs at local level.

The American economist Jeffrey Sachs, who is an adviser to a number of Eastern European countries in the rebuilding stage, believes that the communist economic systems failed before their governments fell. He argues that the Communist economies ran into three simultaneous crises: they were doing the wrong things, they were doing them badly, and they ran out of money.[31] Dealing with women in management was part of what they were doing wrong and badly.

To demonstrate gender conditioning in the West, advocates of equal rights for women developed a classic test. A story was told, presented as a riddle. It went like this:

A man and his 8-year-old son were travelling in a car. As it crossed a railroad track, the car was struck by a train and the man was killed outright. The seriously injured boy was taken to a hospital and carried into the emergency ward. On seeing the boy the chief surgeon said 'I cannot operate on this boy, he's my son!' How is this possible?

Many men and women struggled with the riddle, inventing bizarre story lines to explain the chief surgeon's refusal – all predicated on the assumption that the chief surgeon was a man when, in fact, the answer was simple: the chief surgeon was his mother. The story does not work in the former Soviet Union where chief surgeons are, more often than not, women.

The former Soviet Union has been presented as an ideal case – a country where women were guaranteed equal rights with men under the Constitution, had brilliant technical and professional career prospects, made up slightly more than half the workforce and moreover were celebrated as the protectors of the nation's moral and social values. Further, women were to be full participants in all aspects of the former Soviet Union's society, founded on a grand social design. A department of women's affairs, led by a powerful and respected role model woman, was set up to protect women's interests.

Reality fell far short of the Soviet ideal and its propaganda over the last 70 years. Women were encumbered with fulfilling society's expectations of work outside the home as well as assuming primary responsibility for home and family. Those women aspiring to powerful managerial posts, who had the requisite education and energy, were often blocked by male rivals for the positions in a Soviet version of the glass ceiling.

The policy of glasnost (openness) has opened up a debate on the role of women in Soviet society. A protagonist position in the debate demands increased power and visibility at work for women which would result in greater numbers of women managers.

While president of the Soviet Union, Mikhail Gorbachev said: 'Further democratisation of society, which is the pivot and guarantor of perestroika (restructuring), is impossible without enhancing the role of women, without women's active and specific involvement and without their commitment to our reforming efforts. I am convinced that women's role in our society will steadily grow'.[32]

At the same time Gorbachev supported Soviet efforts to return women to their traditional role of raising a family or, in his words, 'their purely womanly mission'.

Beyond the rhetoric, what remains factual is that women in the former Soviet Union, despite their training and ability, do not hold sufficient numbers of the managerial positions. One reason for this is the 'double burden' of career and family management. Another is the unwillingness of men to share managerial power and control with women. Today women hold only one-tenth of the top managerial jobs. Occupational and wage discrimination against women is widespread as most women work in the poorest sectors of the economy, earning the lowest wages in the most dangerous working conditions. For example, in the Russian republic, about 20 per cent of working women work evening and night shifts and women there perform 58 per cent of industrial manual labour.

Even in jobs traditionally female, such as teaching, there is evidence of sex discrimination. In public education, for example, 81 per cent of the teachers in grades one to ten are women, but only 41 per cent of the principals in elementary schools (grades one to eight) are women and only 36 per cent of secondary schools' principals are women.

According to researcher Sheila M. Puffer, 'Surveys conducted over the past few years show that many Soviet women want to continue working and that a sizeable number seek advancement up the managerial ladder. According to one survey, 60 per cent of women would continue working even if their husbands earned the sum of what they both currently earned.'[33] Ninety per cent of professional women responding to a survey by Soviet psychologists rated their professional and family roles of equal importance.

Puffer presents a five-point plan based on her research to alter the current Soviet situation for women.

1. The creation of an infrastructure of social services to help women cope with family and home tasks.
2. Education to eradicate sex-role stereotypes.
3. Management training for women.
4. Changes in the nature of managerial work to make it more compatible with a woman's other responsibilities.
5. The creation of women's organisations as pressure groups.

The Czechs are widely regarded as role model reformers with a privatisation programme almost completed and low inflation rates. Reform efforts have enjoyed enough wide support to allow the Czech Prime

Minister to boast that they were 'out of the operating theatre and into the recovery room'. However, the question of the number of women chief surgeons and senior managers will remain a controversial one.

# References

1. Pillinger, J. *Feminising the Market, Women's Pay and Employment in the European Community*, Macmillan Press, London, 1992, p. 174.
2. Commission of the European Communities, *Employment in Europe 1993*, Directorate-General, Employment, Industrial Relations and Social Affairs, Brussels.
3. Ibid.
4. Hänninen-Salmelin, E. and Petäjäniemi, T., 'Women managers: the case of Finland' in N. Adler and D. Izraeli (eds), *Competitive Frontiers: Women Managers in a Global Economy*, Blackwell, Cambridge, MA, 1994.
5. *Financial Times*, 3 July 1991, p. 14.
6. Davidson, M. and Cooper, C. (eds), *European Women in Business and Management*, Paul Chapman, London, 1993.
7. *Who's Who in Industry*, Fulcrum Publishing, London, 1991.
8. Antal, A. B. and Krebsbach-Gnath, C., 'Germany' in M. Davidson and C. Cooper (eds), *European Women in Business and Management*, Paul Chapman, London, 1993.
9. Laufer, J., 'France' in M. Davidson and C. Cooper (eds), *European Women in Business and Management*, Paul Chapman, London, 1993.
10. Albertsen, J. and Christensen, B., 'Denmark' in M. Davidson and C. Cooper (eds), *European Women in Business and Management*, Paul Chapman, London, 1993.
11. Central Statistical Office, *Social Trends*, Central Statistics Office, London, 1994.
12. Serdjénian, E., 'Women managers in France' in N. Adler and D. Izraeli (eds), *Competitive Frontiers*, Blackwell, Cambridge, MA, 1994.
13. BBC *Panorama* 'The Future is Female', 24 October, 1994.
14. Beloff, H., survey presented at the British Psychological Society annual conference, in Scarborough, Yorkshire, April 1990.
15. Olivares, F., 'Italy' in M. Davidson and C. Cooper (eds), *European Women in Business and Management*, Paul Chapman, London, 1993.
16. CRORA, *Professional and Personal Profile of Senior Women Managers in Italy*, Centre for Research on Company Organisations, Bocconi University, Milan, 1987.
17. *The Times*, 21 November 1992, p. 15A.
18. Alban-Metcalfe, B. and Nicholson, N., *The Career Development of British Managers*, British Institute of Management Foundation, London, 1984.
19. *Financial Times*, 23 June 1991.
20. Cooper, C. and Lewis, S., *The Workplace Revolution: Managing today's dual career families*, Kogan Page, London, 1993.
21. Tijdens, K., 'The Netherlands in M. Davidson and C. Cooper (eds), *European Women in Business and Management*, Paul Chapman, London, 1993.

22. Hegewisch, A. and Mayne, L., 'Equal opportunity policies in Europe' in C. Brewster and A. Hegewisch (eds), *Policy and Practice of European HRM*, Routledge, London, 1994.
23. Alimo-Metcalfe, B. and Wedderburn-Tate, C., 'The United Kingdom' in M. Davidson and C. Cooper (eds), *European Women in Business and Management*, Paul Chapman, London, 1993.
24. Wolff, Isabel, 'Congratulations – and You're Fired', *Observer*, 20 November 1994.
25. Albertsen, J. and Christensen, B., 'Denmark' in M. Davidson and C. Cooper (eds), *European Women in Business and Management*, Paul Chapman, London, 1993.
26. *The Times*, 1 December 1992, p. 6F.
27. Brewster, C. and Hegewisch, A., *Policy and Practice in European Human Resource Management: the Price Waterhouse Cranfield Survey*, Routledge, London, 1994.
28. Woodward, A., 'Belgium' in M. Davidson and C. Cooper (eds), *European Women in Business and Management*, Paul Chapman, London, 1993.
29. Hammond, V. and Holton, V., 'The scenario for women managers in Britain in the 1990s' in Nancy J. Adler and Dafna N. Izraeli (eds), *Competitive Frontiers, Women Managers in a Global Economy*, Blackwell, Cambridge, MA, 1994.
30. Siemienska, R., 'Women Managers in Poland: In Transition from Communism to Democracy' in Nancy J. Adler and Dafna N. Izraeli (eds), *Competitive Frontiers, Women Managers in a Global Economy*, Blackwell, Oxford, 1994, p. 243.
31. *Understand Shock Therapy*, The Social Market Foundation, London, 1994.
32. Gorbachev, M. S., *Perestroika: New Thinking for our Country and the World*, Harper & Row, New York, 1987.
33. Puffer, S. M., 'Women Managers in the former U.S.S.R.: A case of "Too Much Equality?"' in Nancy H. Adler and Dafna N. Izraeli, *Competitive Frontiers, Women Managers in a Global Economy*, Blackwell, Oxford, 1994, p. 280.

# 2

# Sex Differences

## Nina L. Colwill

Aerodynamically the bumble bee shouldn't be able to fly, but the bumble bee doesn't know it so goes on flying anyway.

Mary Kay Ash

- Do men make better managers than women?[1]
- Do women and men have different abilities?

These questions and hundreds like them have been addressed by researchers in their study of sex differences in organisational behaviour – in their study of men's and women's characteristics and performance. In this chapter the results of this research will be examined – research on sex differences in physical abilities, cognitive abilities, social skills and leadership styles. First, some of the problems inherent in research on sex differences in organisations will be highlighted.

## Research problems and issues

Over the course of our working lives we read many studies, usually second-hand versions, and our perceptions of the differences between men and women receive another boost. But how different are the women and men who seek the same career paths through management, and how might the research methods that business researchers use create sex differences that never, in fact, existed? The following six issues should raise some valid questions.

# 1. The differences orientation

Researchers look for differences: the differences between blacks and whites, supervisors and subordinates, white- and blue-collar workers, and women and men. These studies teach us about the effects of race, of status, of occupation and of sex. Because researchers are interested in differences and publishers publish differences, studies showing sex differences have an edge in the publishing game. Thus, an unknown number of studies that show the sexes to be more alike than different have been relegated to wastepaper bins, giving an erroneous impression of how different the sexes really are.

# 2. Correlation vs. experimentation

There is a reason why sex-differences research is particularly susceptible to problems of interpretation: there are no true experiments in this area. A true experiment requires that a variable be manipulated or that people be randomly assigned to certain groups. These criteria cannot possibly be satisified in sex-differences research. Researchers cannot manipulate people's sex or randomly assign them to male or female groups, so they cannot do true experiments. Instead, they do correlational research, which merely allows them to say that two variables are correlated or related to each other, never that one *causes* the other. Sex is correlated with the ability to type, for instance, but it is no more possible to say that biological sex causes typing skills than to say that typing skills cause biological sex.

Because sex-differences research is always, of necessity, correlational, it is particularly vulnerable to misinterpretation, for sex differences often mask other variables in the research. In Rosabeth Moss Kanter's research, described in her book, *Men and Women of the Corporation*,[2] Kanter sought to understand why women tend to be less successful in business than men, by exploring the background variables that might make women less effective managers. Because she found no consistent patterns, she began to reconceptualise the problem. Perhaps women were not less effective managers at all, she reasoned; perhaps she was confusing sex with organisational position. Perhaps there were situations in the organisation that discouraged strong leadership styles and perhaps women were more likely to be placed in these situations. As it transpired, she was right. Female managers in the multinational conglomerate that Kanter was observing tended to be placed in dead-end positions, token positions and managerial positions in which they were accorded no real power, and men *and* women who found themselves in such positions tended to be bureaucratic rule-keepers rather than strong leaders. The quality of leadership was not determined by sex; it was determined by the organisational resources and organisational support that was accorded to the manager.

Most of what we 'know' about the behaviour of men and women in organisations is based upon our own informal correlational studies – upon our observations of the ways in which biological sex is related to a variety of job-related traits and abilities. Researchers who misinterpret their own data by failing to control for non-sex variables in their studies can provide our sex-role stereotypes with food for growth.

## 3. Sex and status

Closely aligned to the problem of correlational research is a third issue: it is virtually impossible in our society to separate the variables of sex and status, and nowhere is this problem more salient than it is in organisations. In virtually every western country more than 95 per cent of secretaries are female and more than 95 per cent of senior executives are male. Women make less money than men, they give fewer orders than men, and they climb the organisational ladder more slowly than men. To say that women have less status than men is redundant.

So pervasive is the notion that the sexes differ in status that people assign different status to men and women in the same occupation, depending on the sex-role appropriateness of their occupational choice. Furthermore, people of high and low status tend to speak and act differently; and there is strong evidence that men tend to behave as high status people and that women tend to behave as low status people, as will be shown later in this chapter. When researchers fail to control for status in their sex-differences research, it is often impossible to know if we are observing sex differences or status differences.

## 4. Raters: the yardstick problem

Studies in organisational behaviour are often dependent upon raters or judges to describe, measure or evaluate the behaviour of women and men. No matter how well raters are trained and no matter how nonsexist they believe themselves to be, they can never be expected to measure women and men with the same yardstick. There is hardly a behaviour in which women and men can engage to which some sex-role stereotype cannot be attached; hence the tendency to see one sex as behaving sex-role appropriately and the other sex as behaving sex-role inappropriately. Different meanings are attached to the same act, whether it is speaking with authority, engaging in emotional outbursts or keeping a family picture on one's desk. Raters are not magical people who are immune to such sexism – they learnt their stereotypes as well as everyone else did, and they often produce studies that say more about the raters than they do about men and women in organisations.

## 5. Subject–researcher interactions

Most sex-differences studies require a social interaction between the researcher and the people being researched, and social interaction is a veritable breeding ground for research problems. Females tend to be more cooperative research subjects than do males. It also appears that researchers of both sexes treat male and female subjects differently – that research assistants are seen to be 'more likeable, pleasant, friendly, encouraging, honest and relaxed', when they are interacting with females. Robert Rosenthal,[3] who has devoted his research career to studying research methods, has suggested, in fact, that researchers behave so differently to male and female subjects, even when administering the same formally programmed procedures, that male and female subjects may, psychologically, simply not be in the same study at all. If males and females are accorded such differential treatment that they seem to be in different studies, it is not surprising that they are behaving differently and that researchers are finding what they have come to call sex differences.

## 6. Generalisability

The last problem to be mentioned here, but by no means the end of the list, has to do with generalisability. Much of what we 'know' about sex differences in organisational behaviour was studied, not in the organisations to which the behaviour can hopefully be generalised, but in university classrooms and laboratories. The subjects are often introductory psychology students who may obtain some credit for their participation. Whether the same sex differences would be found among male and female managers, however, is the question of interest. Women and men who enter similar training have similar interests, abilities and traits, and their training reinforces those similarities. It would be naïve to believe that male and female managers are no more alike than male and female introductory psychology students. It has been well demonstrated that men are more physically aggressive and less nurturant than women. Is there a sex difference in aggression among wrestlers and a sex difference in nurturance among day-care workers? Because that is what really matters. If we are to move beyond our sex-role stereotypes, we must do high-quality research and read high-quality research. Every reader of this book is a consumer of research, and it is in the best interest of every reader to be an intelligent consumer.

## Physical abilities

Women have long been regarded as the weaker sex. It is true that as a group they are shorter, lighter and less muscular than men. Men's advantage in size and muscular strength has been clearly demonstrated by their performance in athletic competition. In Olympic events in which both sexes participate, men continually outpace women. Interestingly enough, however, the differences between men's and women's records in certain events are decreasing rapidly. Women have always excelled in endurance swimming, in which they hold many world records.[4]

It has long been recognised that men, however more physically large, however more muscular, are constitutionally weaker than females. From the moment of conception and throughout the birth process they are far more vulnerable to injury and death. In childhood they are more often the victims of disease, and throughout their lives are less likely to recover from illness. Starvation, shock, exposure and fatigue have less negative consequences for women than for men, and women's life span is almost universally longer than men's.[5] Even within their physical senses and within their psychological responses to the world, women and men exhibit some differences. Although women lose their reading vision earlier than men, females appear to have more acute taste and hearing and to be more sensitive to touch.[6] Males are more prevalent than are females in the ranks of many psychophysiological disorders such as mental retardation, antisocial personality disorders, attention deficits and pathological gambling, but there are a few psychological conditions, such as eating disorders, in which women are much more likely to be represented.[7] These physical sex differences may have some implications for some men and women in some occupations. But the differences are often so small and the overlap between the sexes so large that there are few practical restrictions for the individual woman or man who wants to enter an occupation requiring any of these physical attributes. Furthermore, the focus of this book is on management, and the characteristics required of managers are usually much more cognitive than physical.

## Cognitive abilities

There is no area in the study of sex differences that has received the research energy that has been devoted to cognitive abilities. Many thousands of studies have been undertaken in this area over a period of many decades, suggesting that everything there is to know about sex differences in cognitive abilities is known. Unfortunately, this is not true. Although there are still as many questions as answers in this complex area, Diane Halpern's recent book, *Sex Differences in Cognitive Abilities*,[8] provides a cogent summary.

Cognitive abilities are usually divided into three specific skills: verbal, visual–spatial and mathematical abilities. Even these three distinctions do not represent three unitary concepts. There are many components to each of these abilities, as will soon be obvious.

## Verbal abilities

Sex differences in verbal abilities are fairly consistent across a wide variety of ages. Among children, girls tend to talk earlier than boys, produce longer and more varied sentences, have larger vocabularies and make fewer errors. Among adults, men tend to have an edge in the solving of analogies, but women outperform men in most other verbal tests, including vocabulary, anagrams and verbal fluency. In addition, females are less likely than males to have verbal problems such as stuttering and dyslexia, are less likely to suffer language impairment from a stroke and recover more quickly if they do.

## Visual–spatial ability

To examine a definition of visual–spatial ability is to wonder if this ability is of any importance, for it is defined as the ability to 'imagine what an irregular figure would look like if it were rotated in space' or 'the ability to discern the relationship among shapes and objects'.[9] Visual–spatial abilities are, however, an important component of human thought and are essential prerequisites for engineers, architects, air crew and builders. Visual–spatial abilities clearly favour males.

Sex differences in visual–spatial ability begin to appear as early as age 7 years – much later than do sex differences in verbal abilities – and they start to become reliable at around age 18 years. For both males and females visual–spatial abilities decline with age, but the sex difference remains. There is, however, a wide variability in performance, particularly among women, making it difficult to predict how well any one woman or man will do. Furthermore, these sex differences do not seem to apply to the everyday skills that should require good visual–spatial performance. Although driving a car is highly dependent upon visual–spatial skills, for instance, females have far fewer accidents than males do. Although a correlation has been found between musical ability and visual–spatial ability few sex differences have been found in musical ability, and those that have been found tend to favour women.

## Mathematical ability

At the upper levels of mathematical ability – among people identified as mathematical geniuses – males predominate. Within the general population, however, sex differences in mathematical ability are less consistent. In general, they begin in elementary schools with an advantage for females and work their way, at around age 17 towards an advantage for males. However, even that much-discussed finding is confusing, particularly in adulthood, where the male advantage decreases substantially when a number of mathematics courses are taken into account. Furthermore, the results are mixed: in tests like mathematical reasoning which are thought to depend partially on verbal skills females tend to do better than males, while males excel in the spatially based mathematical tests of geometry and statistics.

## Interpreting sex differences in cognitive abilities

As Diane Halpern has pointed out, there is a thorny problem in all of this research. There are two types of tests that measure a person's cognitive skills: tests of achievement and tests of ability. *Tests of achievement* measure what a person knows, what a person has learned. University examinations, for example, purport to be tests of achievement. *Tests of ability*, on the other hand, purport to be tests of a person's potential to learn, a measure of a person's ability to benefit from instruction in that area.

Whenever a test is constructed, its scores should ideally be correlated with whatever it is purporting to measure. Tests of mathematical ability, for instance, purport to measure an ability to do mathematics, so a good test of mathematical ability should be related to the ability to do mathematics. *Mathematical ability should predict mathematical achievement.* Unfortunately, it takes a long time to construct tests in that way. One must give a test of mathematical ability to many subjects, then collect their scores in future mathematics courses, and correlate the two scores. Ideally, the researchers should even test the performance of the subjects in mathematically related jobs and correlate those data with the subjects' ability scores, to see if the test is really able to predict job performance in areas such as engineering and construction. However, it is very difficult and expensive to track subjects over time, and not everyone will continue to cooperate. Not everyone will even take mathematics courses, much less work in a mathematics-related area, so in order to find a feasible way to construct a test, psychologists correlate their test of mathematical ability, not with performance in real life but with performance on another test – a test of mathematical achievement. There are very few tests of cognitive ability that have been rigorously constructed; usually their scores have merely been compared to the best thing available at the time – another test.

### Ability vs. achievement

There is another problem associated with ability testing that is relevant here: it is very difficult to measure people's *abilities independent of their achievements*. How does one measure mathematical ability, for example, without asking mathematical questions? And who is in a better position to answer mathematical questions correctly than the person who has studied mathematics, the person who has already achieved in mathematics? Because more men than women study mathematics, and use mathematics in their work, it is not surprising that adult males demonstrate greater mathematical ability than do adult females on tests of mathematical ability.

### Ability vs. motivation

Furthermore, no one has yet discovered a method for testing *ability independent of motivation*. So, for example, if a teenage boy is disinterested in being perceived as a verbally astute person (and he might well be, given the sex-role stereotype of verbal skills being feminine) he is unlikely to apply himself as diligently to the completion of a verbal ability test as would a person who considered verbal ability to be an important skill. His sister, on the other hand, is more likely to be rewarded for verbal ability, and therefore more likely to be motivated to excel in it. Thus a test of verbal ability, like all tests, is partially a test of motivation.

### Ability vs. stereotypes

Just as people who are poorly motivated tend not to do well on a task, so are people less likely to succeed in tasks that they do not consider themselves to be competent to undertake. As individuals, we tend to believe stereotypes about our groups and to apply them to ourselves. If a teenage girl believes that males are more *competent* than females at spatial skills, she is unlikely to see herself as spatially inclined, and less likely to do well on a test of visual–spatial ability. Our stereotypes are formed and reinforced by messages to boys and men that verbal skills are not nearly as important as scientific skills, messages to girls and women that their verbal acuity is more important than their mathematical prowess.

Thus ability tests, the purest measure of cognitive abilities, are still contaminated by testing problems and by a lifetime of messages and experiences that are brought to the testing session. As Diane Halpern says:

> A pure measure of cognitive ability would separate what each of the sexes in fact do (achievement) from what each of the sexes can do (ability). This is not yet possible.[10]

## Social skills

Sex-role stereotypes in the western world label women as the most socially astute of the two sexes. The stereotype, it appears, has some basis in fact. Women smile more than males, engage in more eye contact and are more sensitive to the nonverbal communications of others.[11] To be more socially skilled they must communicate – must give messages to others and must receive messages from others.

There are three ways in which we can communicate with other human beings: verbally (the words said), paraverbally (the way the words are said), and nonverbally (communication without words). There are sex differences in all three ways of communicating.

## Verbal skills[12]

From birth to death females have better verbal skills than males. The different ways in which men and women use their verbal abilities in order to communicate will now be examined. Please note that many of these sex differences reflect and reinforce the status differences between women and men.

### Polite form
Women tend to use more polite forms than do men. They are much more likely to lengthen, and thereby to soften, their requests with such polite phrases as 'Will you please get this letter out in today's post?' or 'Won't you please finish this work before you leave for the day?' This technique often serves to turn requests and commands into questions.

### Tag question
Women are more likely to add tag questions to their statements, giving the impression of uncertainty: 'This report tells us everything we want to know, doesn't it?' or 'She's the best person for the job, don't you think?' An alternate form of the tag question has the speaker making a statement in a questioning voice: 'I'll expect you to have this report ready by Tuesday?'

In either case, the questioning form weakens the speaker's commitment to the statement and implicitly invites confirmation from the person addressed, thereby lowering the speaker's status.

*Qualifiers*
Women are more likely than men to qualify their statements. They are more likely to say '*Perhaps* this is the best solution to the problem', '*I wonder if* we shouldn't fire Tom', or '*I think* we have found a superior product', even in situations in which they know themselves to be knowledgeable and correct.

*Disclaimers*
Women are more likely than men to use disclaimers. They tend to lower the expectations of their audiences with such self-deprecating statements as '*I know this may sound silly*, but have you considered combining the two departments?' or '*I know I'm not an expert*, but I think we should buy the new computer'. (Notice that disclaimers are almost invariably followed by qualifiers like 'have you considered?' or 'I think', that further weaken the position of the speaker.)

*Different words*
Women use many words that are seldom, if ever, included in the male vernacular. Some of these words describe nuances of differences in colour or form seldom articulated by men: words such as 'mauve' or 'ecru'. Others are elaborate, highly descriptive or superlative words such as 'charming', 'adorable' or 'loveliest'. Women also use more exclamatory phrases not considered to be profanity – phrases such as 'Oh dear!' – and more words that imply feeling, evaluation and interpretation. Men, on the other hand, make more references to time, space, quantity, aggression, perception and physical movement and are more likely to use profanity. When their words are analysed for emotional content, women are found to use more supportive language and men to use more hostile verbs.[13]

**The implications**
Someone living on another planet and reading about these sex differences in verbal communication might be forgiven for assuming that women would be represented in larger numbers than men in occupations requiring tact, negotiation and superior social skills – that women would be the executives, the liaison officers and the ambassadors of this planet. However, this has never been the case. Rather, the verbal styles associated with women's speech are not only devalued; there is evidence that they are devalued more for women than for men. The research shows, for instance, that women who use tag questions and disclaimers are seen as less intelligent and less knowledgeable: not only less intelligent and less

knowledgeable than *women who do not* use these 'feminine' verbal styles, but less intelligent and less knowledgeable than *men who do* use them.[14]

Not all or even most of our communication takes place verbally. How do men and women differ in their paralanguage – in the way they say the words they say? How do they differ in the ways in which they communicate without words?

## Paraverbal language

Paraverbal communication refers to the way we say the words we say, and again women and men differ substantially. Men's voices tend to be deeper and louder than women's and, contrary to the sex-role stereotype of the chattering female, they tend to talk more. In fact, virtually all the research on mixed-sex groups indicates that men talk more often, use more words to say what they want to say and make more summarising and orientating comments. Men interrupt people more often than women and the people they are most likely to interrupt are women. Women, playing their reciprocal role, are more likely than men to allow themselves to be interrupted. Also consistent with their sex role, women are more likely than men to play a nurturing, head-nodding role in mixed-sex groups.[15]

### Long-term effects

Most of the research that examines sex differences in verbal and paraverbal communication could be legitimately criticised for the fact that it focuses on first impressions. Strangers are brought together to interact in mixed-sex groups or men and women are asked to evaluate a short audiotape or videotape of men's and women's verbal and paraverbal behaviours. There is one study, however, that examined the communication styles of women and men over a 15-week period as they engaged in lengthy group discussions of contemporary business problems.[16] Although many of their results are similar to those found in the broader research literature, there is one subtle and promising finding.

The men who took part in the discussions that formed this study were more likely than the women to use informal and third-person pronouns, imperatives, slang and aggressive language. They tended to reference authoritative sources in their arguments, to interrupt the women and to change topic. Their conversations often focused on competition, control, aggression and violence. Women, on the other hand, tended towards communication styles that would foster participation and communication. They self-disclosed more than the men did and used more personal references and emotional tone and language. They tended to listen more actively, rephrasing ideas and asking for clarification. Often, during the 15 weeks that the study ran, women tried to help competitors to reach a consensus.

These results, as mentioned earlier, are similar, if more detailed, than the results found in many of the first-impressions studies of verbal and paraverbal interactions. There is, however, one finding that goes beyond these more restricted studies: the most influential members of the group were the men and women who adapted some features of the communication styles of the other sex. Thus, the most effective men softened their speech with tag questions and qualifications and changed topics less abruptly than did their male peers. They were more self-disclosing than the other men and expressed their feelings more readily. The most effective women used more slang, more third-person pronouns and longer, more complex sentences. They refused to be interrupted and they used a technique often adapted by leaders in a group: that of speaking to the group as a whole rather than to the person who asked the last question or made the last comment.

The results of this study are extremely promising, because they demonstrate how positive, non-offensive communication styles that are typically used by one sex can be effectively used by the other sex. Hopefully they are pointing towards a day when effective communication is a thoughtful and articulate process, no longer sex-specific.

## Nonverbal communication

When giving communications seminars I often use different types of body language and ask participants which sex performs which gesture. People laugh with recognition when they take part in this exercise and rarely do they make a mistake. We all know about the nonverbal communication styles of women and men, for we see them every day, but rarely do we articulate them.

Men are more likely than women to perform an act called 'steepling' – to touch their fingertips together while they rest their elbows on a flat surface such as a desk. The message this conveys is one of superior knowledge. In all the many times I have asked students and managers to identify the sex of the person who performs this act, no one has ever attributed it to women.

Women, on the other hand, perform other familiar gestures. They are more likely to sit and stand with their legs together, taking up as little space as possible, exhibiting what used to be called 'ladylike behaviour'. Men are more likely to use more physical space than their size would suggest that they require, often invading the physical space of others, particularly women. Perhaps because we tend to 'touch down' in our society and women are so often in positions of lower status than men, men are more likely to touch women than vice versa.

Our eyes are famous for their communication abilities and women are more likely than men to stare at people who are not looking at them and to avert their gaze when speaking to others. Men, on the other hand, are more likely to 'look people in the eye'. Of course, eye contact is a learned behaviour and women are learning it quickly as they attain higher status and more leadership roles in today's organisations.

# Leadership styles[17]

During recent years two different and conflicting bodies of literature have emerged in the study of sex differences in leadership style. One view, represented in popular management books, suggests that women and men employ very different leadership styles. In these books, data are drawn primarily from the organisational experiences of the authors and from their interviews with a limited number of managers. Men's styles are seen to be more competitive, controlling, unemotional, analytical and hierarchical; women's styles tend to be presented as more collaborative and co-operative.

The second body of literature is based primarily on the research of social scientists. Reviews in this area tend to focus on small samples of research articles, and usually come to the same conclusion: there are no consistent sex differences in leadership styles.

Faced with these conflicting reports, Alice Eagly and Blair Johnson[17] undertook a review of the literature in which they analysed studies of men's and women's leadership styles. There were a total of 370 comparisons made: 289 in natural organisational settings, 56 in assessment situations and 25 in laboratory studies. They examined studies of self-reported leadership styles and studies in which the managers were rated by their supervisors, their subordinates, their peers and independent judges. The average age of these managers was early to late thirties, and they occupied positions ranging from first-line supervision to top management. By examining the 370 comparisons undertaken in these two studies, the authors concluded that:

1. 'The strongest evidence ... for a sex difference in leadership style occurred on the tendency for women to adopt a more *democratic* or participative style and for men to adopt a more *autocratic* or directive style ... 92% of the available comparisons went in the direction of more democratic behaviour from women than men.' The researchers attributed this sex difference, which occurred in organisations, in assessment situations and in the laboratory, primarily to women's greater interpersonal skills and interpersonal complexity.

2. In studies conducted in assessment and laboratory settings male

managers tended to be more *task-orientated* than female managers – better able to organise activities in the interest of performing tasks. However, in studies conducted in their natural organisational settings there were no sex differences among managers in task orientation.

3. In studies conducted in assessment and laboratory settings, female managers tended to be more *interpersonally orientated* than male managers – better at tending to the morale and welfare of other people in the work setting. However, in their natural organisational settings there were no sex differences among managers in interpersonal orientation.

It seems, then, that there are sex differences in leadership style, in task orientation and in interpersonal orientation that are consistent with stereotypes and with popular management books. However, these sex differences are found primarily in laboratory and assessment centre research, and rarely in real organisations with real managers in the act of performing their daily functions. Yet, there is one sex difference that tends to be maintained in a variety of research situations: in the majority of studies women were found to adopt a more democratic or participative style, and men a more autocratic one.

# Conclusion

The research continues. The sex-differences-in-management research has many gaps – gaps that are being filled by researchers who realise that people differ according to their circumstances as surely as they differ according to their sex. People change. People learn. People with similar characteristics seek similar workplace situations and the workplace renders them even more similar, regardless of their sex. It would be pleasant to believe that women and men receive equal treatment as a function of these similarities, but it is clear from the research reviewed in this book that this is not the case. In filling the research gaps, today's researchers are striving to preserve the complexity of all these issues in their study of sex differences in management – in their study of sex and circumstance.

# Notes and References

1. This section on research methods appeared in a slightly different form In Colwill, Nina L., 'On evaluating the research', *Business Quarterly*, Winter, 1982, pp. 19–21.
2. Kanter, Rosabeth Moss, *Men and Women of the Corporation*, Basic Books, New York, 1977.

3. Rosenthal, Robert, *Experimenter Effects in Behavioral Research*, Irvington Publishers, New York, 1976.
4. Lips, Hilary M. and Colwill, Nina L., *The Psychology of Sex Differences*, Prentice-Hall Inc., Englewood Cliffs, NJ, 1978.
5. Montague, Ashley, *The Natural Superiority of Women*, Collier Books, New York, 1968.
6. Baher, M. A. (ed.), *Sex Differences in Human Performance*, Wiley, Chichester, 1987.
7. American Psychological Association, *Diagnostic and Statistical Manual of Mental Disorders*, 3rd edn, APA, Washington, DC, 1987.
8. Halpern, Diane F., *Sex Differences in Cognitive Abilities*, 2nd edn, Lawrence Erlbaum Associates, Hillsdale, NJ, 1992.
   For anyone wishing to attain a sophisticated understanding of the ways in which males and females differ in visual-spatial, verbal, and mathematical skills, Diane Halpern's book is a comprehensive and readable source. With more than 500 references, she examines sex differences in cognitive abilities from a variety of perspectives and has managed to maintain the complexity of this area while writing clearly and simply. In writing this section, I have relied completely on this author.
9. Ibid., p. 68.
10. Ibid., p. 11.
11. See, for a review: Colwill, Nina L., 'Traits, and abilities and their measurement' in Nina L. Colwill, *The New Partnership: Women and Men in Organizations*, Mayfield Publishing Company, Palo Alto, CA, 1982.
12. This section on verbal ability borrows, almost verbatim, from the review: Colwill, Nina L. and Sztaba, Teresa I., 'Organizational genderlect: The problem of two different languages', *Business Quarterly*, Spring, 1986, pp. 64–6.
13. Hyde, J. S., *Half the Human Experience: The Psychology of Women*, 3rd edn, D. C. Heath, Lexington, MA, 1985.
14. Bradley, P. H., 'The folk-linguistics of women's speech: An empirical investigation', *Communication Monographs*, vol. 48, 1981, pp. 73–90.
15. See, for a much more detailed review: Spinner, Barry and Colwill, Nina L., 'Communication' in Nina L. Colwill, *The New Partnership: Women and Men in Organizations*, Mayfield Publishing Company, Palo Alto, CA, 1982.
16. Case, Susan Schnick, 'The collaborative advantage: The usefulness of women's language to contemporary business problems', *Business and the Contemporary World, V*, vol. 3, 1993, pp. 81–105.
17. This section on leadership style summarises the results of what I would consider to be the most comprehensive review in the area: Eagly, Alice H. and Johnson, Blair T., 'Gender and leadership style: A meta-analysis', *Psychological Bulletin* vol. 108, no. 2, 1990, pp. 233–56.

# 3

# Work and the Family

## Aria L. Day and Nina L. Colwill

> The reasons husbands and wives do not understand each other
> is because they belong to different sexes.
>
> Dorothy Dix

People have been studying the interplay of work and family since the time of the ancient Greeks.[1] With the onset of the industrial revolution, however, the separation between work and nonwork was sharply delineated. Work came to be equated with paying work – for the most part, the work that men did. Work and nonwork were considered to be distinct entities, with little or no impact of one domain on the other. It was possible to maintain this separation because of a predominantly male workforce with wives at home to undertake the 'nonwork' family responsibilities: house cleaning, laundry, cooking, organising and child-care.

Over the last 30 years, however, the 'myth of separate (work and nonwork) worlds' has been challenged.[2] One of the biggest catalysts for this challenge is the increasing number of women (especially women with young children) entering the workforce. In trying to balance work and family responsibilities, these women have found it impossible to segregate the two domains. Furthermore, the increasing number of single parent families, the increased longevity of people and the increased emphasis placed on deinstitutionalisation of the elderly have left many people in the 'sandwich generation'. These sandwiched people face the dual challenge of caring for both their children and their parents, while simultaneously developing their careers – often without a spouse to share the load. Moreover, the increasing mobility of workers has meant the loss of traditional nuclear family support.

In addition to these societal and demographic changes, there has been a shift in the way people view work and the value they place on their work and on their family. People are increasingly interested in the quality of their work and family lives and in their ability to maintain a comfortable balance between these two worlds. A study by *Fortune* of 500 managers, for instance, shows that there is an increase in the number of men who want to spend more time with their families.[3]

This chapter begins with an exploration of the various components of the 'family side' of the work–family relationship: the myriad household and child-care responsibilities that dual-career parents face every day. Then we examine the multiple roles that people assume in their work and family lives, the consequences of holding these multiple roles and the many relationships that exist between work and family. The individual factors and the work-related factors that affect work–family relationships are explored next. Finally, we will review some of the organisational and governmental programmes and policies that have been implemented in Europe in an attempt to create a comfortable balance between work and family.

## Housework, roles and satisfaction

When examining the relationship between work and family, researchers and writers have all too often ignored or underestimated the time and effort involved in housework and child-care and the inequity of the distribution of labour in the home. In *The Basset Report*,[4] however, Isabel Basset undertook a comprehensive examination of housework in the dual-career Canadian family.

Among Basset's respondents both spouses agreed that women were bearing the heaviest burden of housework, although husbands' and wives' versions of the time they allocated to housework differed slightly. We have averaged their time estimations here:

- In only 50 per cent of the households did men do *any* cleaning or grocery shopping. (More recent British figures show the same percentage.[5])
- In only one-third of households did husbands do *any* cooking or laundry. (The more recent British figures show this percentage to be 50 per cent.)
- In only one-third of households did women do *any* household repairs.

Men's commitment to household repairs may give an impression of equity until one considers the time spent repairing the average home.

Unless their house is in an extreme state of disrepair, most families devote far more time to cleaning, cooking, laundry, and grocery shopping than they do to household repairs, and most of these chores are done by women. It is also important to remember that Basset's list did not include gift-buying, decorating (which goes far beyond household repairs), planning, hosting, the buying and repairing of clothing and errand-running, let alone child-care. The most recent studies show that in only 10 per cent of Canadian families do husbands and wives say that they share equally in household chores.[6]

It might be assumed that women would be rioting in the streets over inequalities in the distribution of housework. Occasionally we hear of a dramatic revolt, such as the one-day women's strike in Iceland, but by and large there are very few complaints. In one study, for instance, university faculty women acknowledged that they spent less time on their careers and more time on household and child-care responsibilities than did their husbands,[7] yet these same women did not believe that their marriages were inequitable. However, it is not clear if these women were unaware of the inequities or if they did not consider the traditional household division of labour by sex to be unfair.

Perhaps they are too tired to care. There is an intuitive appeal to the notion that the multiple roles and responsibilities of dual-career mothers may lead to stress and, ultimately, to poor mental and physical health. Given the complex work lives of dual-career women and the housework and child-care inequalities they are likely to face at home, it is easy to imagine that these multiple roles would at least create role conflict and role overload. It is equally easy to imagine that this role conflict and role overload would generate enough anger and frustration to affect negatively the work lives and the personal lives of these women, but the data[8] simply do not support this contention.

Although *employed women* are more likely than other women to say that they feel rushed, they do not report significantly more stress than do their unemployed counterparts. Furthermore, employed women report higher self-esteem and greater feelings of satisfaction and personal control. Although *single employed mothers* report greater stress and less satisfaction than other women, women who combine the three roles of *mother, wife and wage-earner* tend to report fewer chronic conditions and short-term symptoms, feel healthier and use fewer prescription drugs than other women. In one study of 1232 Los Angeles women,[9] role conflict and role overload appeared to be overshadowed by the rewards inherent in their multiple roles. Among these women, in fact, married and cohabiting women were the group most likely to describe themselves as being 'very satisfied' with their work, and never-married women were those most likely to describe themselves as 'very dissatisfied'. (Incidentally, it appears that women's health problems are likely to be created by the effects of chronic stress, unhappiness and dissatisfaction rather than the effects of time pressures and acute stresses.)

Although these results appear to run contrary to common sense Lois Verbugge, who has researched in this area for two decades, explains the seeming discrepancy by emphasising the multiple impact of multiple roles: 'social ties and support, responsibilities and obligations, use of skills, and access to resources – factors that can enrich or tax women's lives'.[10]

It appears, then, that dual-career mothers are the happiest, healthiest and most satisfied of women. If that is the case, why do so many female managers forego marriage and family? This apparent sacrifice on the part of female managers suggests that the relationship between their work and family lives may be affected by job characteristics as well as by individual characteristics. Before these variables are examined, however, it is necessary to review the various types of work and family relationships.

# Work–family relationships

It is clear that the literature on dual-career families will always be fraught with a complexity of problems. Despite the fact that many people are faced with similar work and family responsibilities, the work–family relationship may be experienced differently from one person to the next.

## Evans and Bartolome's work–family relationships

Researchers[11] have suggested that there are at least six different types of work–family relationships: independent, spillover, conflict, compensation, instrumental and integrative.

### Independent
Rhonda leaves the house at 8.15 a.m., after her two children have boarded the school bus, and leaves the office at 4.30 p.m., half an hour before they reach home. Rhonda has an ex-directory telephone number and no one from the office has ever called her at home. In the five years she has worked in London, she has never made nor received a personal telephone call; she has never attended an office party; she has never worked overtime; and she has never missed a day of work. Rhonda's children do not quite understand what she does for a living and some of her colleagues do not know that she is married. That is the way she likes it.

For Rhonda, work and family are completely independent. However, few people today are able to maintain such complete independence between their work and their family lives. Rhonda's husband, Jim, is a good example.

## Spillover

Jim is a sculptor who usually works at home and is the primary caretaker for their children, Laura and Alex. The family have just returned home from Jim's opening at the local art gallery where Laura, Alex and Rhonda have been busy greeting and serving the guests. Jim received rave reviews and is basking in his success. He has promised to take them out for dinner the next evening to thank them for their support. However, Alex and Laura look flushed, and they begin to complain of stomach aches. Jim realises that the dinner plans may have to be postponed and that his work plans for tomorrow may have to be cancelled as he cares for two sick children. 'I hope I don't have to miss the meeting with the gallery administrators on Thursday', he thinks.

Jim's situation exemplifies some of the positive and negative ways that work and family spill into each other. His family life spills positively into his work life, as his family helps him at the gallery reception. Moreover, he is experiencing positive work-to-family spillover, as his work success creates a positive mood that carries over to his family life. He is anticipating negative family-to-work spillover, however, as he deals with the possibility of missing work while he cares for his sick children.

## Conflict

Jennifer forever feels that she is operating in the middle of chaos. She is talking to herself again: 'I'd take this work home if my mother-in-law weren't coming for dinner. This is the third time this month I've worked late when she was visiting. She'll think I never make dinner. I have to go home. I'd better get as much done as I can before 5 o'clock. Maybe Robert will do the lion's share on this report. Oh no! There's the phone.

'Jennifer Henderson. Hello, Robert; I was just going to call you. Oh no! Of course, Robert, go! No, don't worry about the report. I'll finish it. Your father needs you there. No, don't worry, just go. I'll talk to you later in the week. And, Robert, I'm sorry about your father.'

'Hello, Mother. It's Jennifer. Look, Mother, I know I've invited you over for dinner tonight, but . . .'

That is work–family conflict.

## Compensation

Donald and Rebecca do not seem to like each other very much, but they never find the time to discuss the logistics of separating, much less to go for marital counselling. Besides, they do not see each other very often. Rebecca works in the office from nine to five, making contacts, writing orders, servicing old clients and soaking up the admiration of her colleagues. She is her company's top salesperson and every night is a client night. On the few nights that Donald is home, he is working on reports or lounging in front of the television, watching sport. Most of the time he is travelling, creating excellent public relations for his company around the globe. He has received three promotions in three years – a company record – and the managing director has hinted that he is being groomed for a directorship.

Donald often thinks about his brother Murray and his wife, Leonora. They *must* envy him and Rebecca, he thinks. Neither of them have much ambition, of course, but Murray was hurt and bitter when he was passed over for promotion by a man ten years his junior. And that job of Leonora's has absolutely no future.

Murray and Leonora have a wonderful family. And three little grandchildren! They all went to Florida for Christmas. They certainly have fun together and they deserve it; Murray and Leonora have devoted their lives to their children. They sent them all to university. Too bad their own careers had not been more satisfying.

Both these relationships are examples of compensation. Donald and Rebecca are compensating for their unhappy marriage and Murray and Leonora for their unhappy work lives.

## Instrumental

Maria and Luc have never been satisfied with their chosen careers, but they do not want to make a change because they would have a difficult time finding the high pay and job security that their present positions afford them. Because of their jobs, their daughters are able to attend private schools. Their elder daughter has had a passion for riding horses since she was able to walk. Maria and Luc have just bought her a new hunter that she can ride in local events. Their younger daughter started dance lessons two years ago and is showing great promise. She has just been accepted into a prestigious summer dancing programme in France.

The girls' hobbies are expensive, but Maria and Luc earn enough money to support their activities. After all, that is why they work; their work is merely an instrument for creating a satisfying family life.

## Integrative

Prabha and Bernward have lived and worked together for ten years. They started their own company soon after they met, and now own the country's fastest-growing manufacturer and distributor of toys and games.

Both Prabha and Bernward come from large families and they employ many of their relatives, including Prabha's son and Bernward's daughter. It gives them a strong feeling of security to work with people they know so well. They particularly relish the opportunity to provide their older children with career starts. Perhaps they will take over the company when Bernward and Prabha retire.

Prabha and Bernward have a 6-year-old son, Raymond who, with his nanny, has travelled with them extensively. Raymond should have started school this year, but his nanny is a qualified teacher, and they have decided to keep him with them for two more years. They have had some wonderful working holidays together and they are not ready to give them up yet. Their son has a world perspective that he could never hope to gain in the classroom and they enjoy a family lifestyle that they could not afford in their first marriages. Besides, Raymond has proved to be an ideal market tester of foreign toys.

Prabha and Bernward have created a work–family relationship that is integrative. Their work life and family life is inextricably intertwined, just as they often are for farm families and for the owners of small corner shops. Even in businesses as traditional as these, and in families with few unusual circumstances, there are few people who would describe their family as a pure case of any of the six work–family types.

## The complexity of work–family relationships

We see that the relationships between work and family can differ greatly from family to family and from individual to individual. Moreover, there are a number of individual- and work-related factors that can influence the type of work–family relationship that people experience. It appears, for instance, that one's feelings towards one's work has a profound impact on the extent to which work problems spill into the home. In a large study of male managers,[12] those with:

- *positive* feelings towards their jobs, tended to view the work–family relationship as either conflicting or independent;
- *mixed* feelings about work, tended to feel that work spilled into the family domain in a negative manner;
- *negative* work feelings, viewed work as being instrumental – as merely giving them the things they wanted for their family.

Moreover, among managers who felt that work was *very important*, there tended to be a view that the work–family relationship was in conflict or that work spilled into the family setting. Managers who felt that work was *moderately important*, tended to see work and family as being independent of each other. Finally, among managers for whom work was *of little importance*, work was viewed as being instrumental for the family or family life was seen as compensating for the work area.

Personal attitudes may also influence the work–family relationship. In one study of dual-career families,[13] lower conflict among self, parental, spousal and professional roles was associated with higher self-esteem, more pro-feminist attitudes and higher career commitment. This finding, which was consistent for both men and women, is a statement of the complexity of issues that come to bear in the balance between work and family.

Almost every member of a single-parent or dual-career family experiences some work–family interaction, whether positive, negative or both. In fact only among 'independent' people, such as Rhonda described above, do the two areas fail to overlap. There was a time not long ago when most men experienced independent work and family lives, but today there are fewer men and even fewer women for whom these two primary areas of life do not overlap. How are today's organisations addressing this overlap?

# Help from external sources

Although many dual-career couples and single-parent employees feel that they struggle alone in a world in which time is always at a premium, there have been advances in the past 20, 10 and even 5 years. The governments of many countries and thousands of organisations have made great strides in their recognition of the fact that most employees have a life beyond their organisation and that the quality of life often determines the quality of their work.

## What are organisations doing?

Responding to the increased concerns of their employees who are trying to balance work and family, employers have implemented a diverse array of 'family-responsive' programmes and policies. Although the programmes presented in this chapter are only a fraction of the work–family practices in place in today's organisations, they are among the most widely implemented.

Flexitime is the best-known type of programme designed to help alleviate work–family conflict. Flexitime, an example of which is shown in Table 3.1, allows some variation in the starting and quitting times of the work day. There are, however, many variations in the implementation of flexitime, ranging in the degree of flexibility they offer employees. There are other working arrangements that may help reduce work–family conflict: a compressed work week (e.g. four ten-hour days per week), telecommuting, working seasonal hours, part-time employment, and job-sharing with one or more people.

Child-care programmes have also sparked a great deal of public interest recently. When people think of organisational involvement in child-care,

**Table 3.1** A standard form of flexitime.

| Flexitime band | Core time | Flexitime band | Core time | Flexible band |
|---|---|---|---|---|
| 6.30–9.00 | 9.00–11.00 | 11.00–13.00 | 13.00–15.00 | 15.00–17.30 |

however, their first thought is usually of an on-site, company-sponsored day-care centre. While some organisations have chosen this option, many others are financially incapable of providing this benefit. Instead, many organisations have addressed the child-care issue through other programmes: referral services for existing day-care centres, direct and indirect financial subsidies and lobbying for increased availability of child-care in the community.

Another organisational policy that has gained popularity is a flexible-benefit plan or 'cafeteria-style' benefits. This type of policy allows employees to have some choices about their total compensation in one of two ways. Employees may choose the types of benefits they would prefer from a limited number of options; or they may choose the ratio of cash-to-benefits that suits their personal situation, forgoing an extensive benefit plan in order to receive extra pay, for example.

There is a variety of reasons why company directors might choose to implement family-responsive programmes in their organisations. When asked, the majority of managers mention the recruiting advantage, the increased productivity and the reduced rate of absenteeism and tardiness. They also suggest that participatory and people-orientated management styles increase under a family-responsive philosophy, that their company image improves, and that they are able to use these programmes to compensate well-qualified employees who have few promotion opportunities.[14] It is also commonly believed by managers that such programmes reduce stress, accidents and turnover, and that they increase morale and quality of work.[15]

Although some researchers have attempted to quantify the 'family-responsiveness' of organisations, it is not an easy task. Two organisations, both defining themselves as family-responsive or family-orientated, may be providing quite different services. Organisation A, for example, may provide employees with flexible arrival and departure times, while Organisation B provides day-care, flexitime and flexible benefits. Both organisations are considered to be responsive by the standard definition, even though Organisation B is providing more services for its employees. We should also bear in mind that the definitions used within these policies may vary greatly. Flexitime, for example, can mean a permanently scheduled half-hour variation in arrival and departure time or it can mean that the employee is allowed to assume a variable and flexible schedule that requires attendance only for minimal 'core hours'.

Not only are the components of family responsiveness difficult to define, but few companies keep the records and collect the data that would allow researchers to examine the cost–benefit analysis of family responsiveness. Few researchers have undertaken the Herculean task of matching comparable organisations and employees in order to examine the workplace differences among employees in flexible and traditional systems. In the few studies that have been conducted,[16] however, the following results have been found:

- less work–family stress among employees on flexitime schedules;
- a decrease in rates of absenteeism among on-site day-care users;
- a decrease in turnover rates after the implementation of a day-care centre; and
- a belief among employees that the sensitivity and flexibility of supervisors is more important than are organisational policies.

Although some members of the private sector have helped to improve their own reputation and the reputation of business in general by addressing the work-and-family concerns of their employees, there are many who have not. For that reason, few governments have relied solely on the initiatives of the business community and many have implemented work–family policies themselves.

# Conclusion

The past two decades have witnessed profound work–family changes in attitudes, policies and legislation. For some people the pace of this change has been dizzying. For others, particularly for women intent on climbing the organisational ladder, the work–family interface is changing all too slowly.

Ironically, there are cases in which legislation aimed at helping men and women achieve equality at work and at home have actually helped to widen the gap. In Sweden, for instance, both spouses have had equal opportunities to be financially supported by the government while they care for their children, yet their division of labour by sex is one of the most traditional in Europe.[17] As in families all over the world, Swedish men tend to have more highly paid and prestigious jobs than their wives, and women are therefore more likely to be the ones who take part time work and long absences from the workplace. The legislation aimed at creating a sex-role-liberated Sweden came at a time when the most plentiful entry positions were in low-status service areas and many women who filled these positions were married to men whose jobs were better paying and more prestigious and were given top priority in the family. Thus the women who took advantage of these government programmes tended to be seen as being less committed to the workplace than were their husbands, and the stereotypes that created workplace inequalities flourished. Add to this the fact that men receive little external support for their decision to enter into an equal partnership with their wives, and it is not difficult to see why positive change is coming so slowly.

As sex-role-liberation detractors have been saying for decades, 'you can't legislate respect'. It is virtually impossible, in a democratic society, to see that every home and workplace is run under the principles of equity, but the policies, the programmes and the legislation are important first steps. As Olaf Palme noted a quarter of a century ago, we must recognise the equal worth of all human beings – males, females, adults and children – in order to support our legislation and to create new work-and-family realities for ourselves and for our children. The interface between work and family is no longer a 'women's issue'. It is an issue that must be jointly addressed by women and men, the governments of their countries and the organisations in which they work.

# References

1. Wilensky, H., 'Work, careers, and social integration', *International Social Science Journal*, vol. 7, no. 4, 1960, pp. 543–60.
2. Kanter, R. M., *Men and Women of the Corporation*, Basic Books, New York, 1977.
3. Chapman, F. S., 'Executive guilt: Who's taking care of the children?' *Fortune*, 16 February 1987, pp. 30–7.
4. Basset, Isabel, *The Basset Report: Career Success and Canadian Women*, Collins, Toronto, 1985.
5. 'Changing roles slow in coming to Britain', *Women in Management*, vol. 4, no. 1, 1994, p. 8.
6. 'A woman's work is never done: "Shocking" new statistics reveal', *Brandon Sun*, 10 January 1994, p. 1.
7. Yogev, S., 'Do professional women have egalitarian marital relationshps?' *Journal of Marriage and the Family*, vol. 43, 1981, pp. 865–71.
8. Verbrugge, Lois M., 'Marriage matters: Young women's health' in Bonita C. Long and Sharon E. Kahn (eds), *Women, Work, and Coping*, McGill-Queen's University Press, Montral and Kingston, London, Buffalo, 1993, pp. 170–92.
9. Valdez, Roberta L. and Gutek, Barbara A., 'Family roles: A help or a hindrance for working women' in Barbara A. Gutek and Laurie Larwood (eds), *Women's Career Development*, Sage Publications, Newbury Park, 1987, pp. 157–69.

10. Verbugge, op. cit., p. 185.
11. Evans, P. and Bartolome, F., 'The changing pictures of the relationship between career and family', *Journal of Occupational Behaviour*, vol. 5, 1984, pp. 9–21.
12. Ibid.
13. Holahan, C. K. and Gilbert, L. A., 'Conflict betweeen major life roles: Women and men in dual career couples', *Human Relations*, vol. 32, no. 6, 1979, pp. 451–567.
14. Friedman, D. E., *Family-Supportive Policies: The Corporate Decision-Making Process*, The Conference Board, New York, 1987.
15. Friedman, D. E., 'Child care for employees' kids', *Harvard Business Review*, April–March 1986, pp. 28–34.
16. Marquart, J. M., 'How does the employer benefit from child care?' In J. S. Hyde and M. J. Essex (eds), *Parental Leave and Child Care: Setting a Research and Policy Agenda*, Temple University Press, Philadelphia, 1991, pp. 229–45.
17. Colwill, Nina L., and Czarniawska-Joerges, Barbara, 'Sweden's families and Sweden's workplace', *Business Quarterly*, November 1986, pp. 93–5.

# 4

# Women in Management: Power and Powerlessness[1]

## Nina L. Colwill

To deny we need and want power is to deny that we hope to
be effective.

Liz Smith

There was a time when many of us believed that education was the only
barrier separating women from the managerial ranks of government and
business. If women only had professional degrees; if women only had
MBAs; if women only had access to the entry-level positions that would
slowly lead them into management. There were others who believed that
real change would occur only through the education of women *and* men,
through massive attitude change. So we set about the task of writing books
and articles, teaching courses and giving seminars to anyone who cared
to read and listen and to many who did not. All over the world, women
entered into the training and education that would prepare them for
managerial equality with men. Women had only to prove themselves
competent, we believed in those days, and the world would prove itself
to be fair.

Today we are older and wiser. The research energy of hundreds of
academics has been devoted to the study of women, men and organisations. The work of these researchers has been presented at conferences
and published in academic journals and popular magazines. Books have
flowed from publishing houses. Many women have earned their MBAs.
They have entered the professions in unprecedented numbers in what they
believe to be the first step towards leadership. Women have read the
books, earned the credentials and proved their competence. Yet in every
country, in virtually every occupation, in almost every company, women

47

continue to be underrepresented in management in proportion to their representation in the workforce.

Clearly, women have not failed to educate themselves with the intellectual tools of their trades and clearly they have not failed in their attempts to present their cases with eloquence and articulation. If aspiring female managers and those who would support them have failed at anything, they have failed to understand power.

In this chapter we will begin by defining power and move into an exploration of our three definitions: personal power (feeling in control), interpersonal power (influencing others) and organisational power (mobilising resources). We will then look specifically at the paradoxes of power faced daily by women in management.

# Defining power

During the past 15 years I have asked hundreds of women and men in business seminars in Europe and North America to describe the most powerful person they know. Their descriptions differ widely, to be sure, but the most common picture is that of a man, a rather unpleasant man. When asked if they like their most powerful person or if they want to be more like their most powerful person, more than half of the people who have completed this exercise have said 'no'.

However, power wears many faces, some of them highly positive, as this chapter suggests. Whether we like powerful people, fear powerful people or misunderstand powerful people, there are as many definitions of power as there are people who have defined it. Over the years, as I have repeated this exercise in a variety of contexts, I have come to realise that the descriptions fall into three categories:

First, at the individual level, we have: *personal power*, feeling in control of one's own environment, feeling good about oneself. Personal power is essentially the belief that one is powerful.

*Interpersonal power* is power viewed at a one-to-one rather than a purely individual level: 'The ability to get another person to do or to believe something he or she would not necessarily have done or believed spontaneously'[2] – the ability to influence others.

Finally, at the most macro level, we look at the ways in which the individual interacts with the organisation in order to create *organisational power*: 'The ability to mobilize resources; the ability to get things done'.[3]

Thus, personal power is a belief (that one is powerful), interpersonal power is an ability (to influence others) and organisational power is another ability (to mobilise organisational resources).

Each of these types of power can be viewed as being independent and distinct. It is possible, for instance, to effectively mobilise the resources of an organisation yet not to feel in control of one's environment – to have high organisational power with low personal power. It is also possible to exert considerable influence on the people around us, yet to have difficulty mobilising organisational resources – to be interpersonally powerful but not organisationally powerful. So, while the three types of power do tend to reinforce and enhance each other, we will treat them as three separate concepts and examine the differences and similarities of women and men as they experience personal, interpersonal and organisational power in their working lives.

This chapter is based on the premise that female and male managers face a power differential. First, in the area of personal power, although women in general tend to feel less powerful than men in general, male and female managers are equally likely to feel in control of their own environments. In the realm of interpersonal power, the research suggests that female managers are less effective than their male counterparts – that they are less able than men to influence others. In the area of organisational power the latest research indicates that a shift is taking place, and that many people consider female managers to be more effective than male managers at mobilising organisational resources.

# Personal power

Personal power is a belief – the belief that we are in control of our own environment. To have personal power is to feel good about ourselves, to feel comfortable in our own skins. There is a psychological concept called *internal–external locus of control* (I–E) that comes very close to defining the notion of personal power. I–E is a measure of the extent to which we believe ourselves to be in control of our environment. To be *internal*, according to Julian Rotter,[4] who brought us the concept and the measure over quarter of a century ago, is to believe that one's destiny is determined by one's own efforts and endeavours. To be *external* is to believe that one's fate is in the hands of luck or chance or powerful others.

Rotter and his followers conceptualised I–E as a personality characteristic, but many other people, including myself, see it as a belief. A personality characteristic is relatively stable. We do not change our personalities by changing our minds. We do not readily learn a new personality; but a belief, on the other hand, is within our conscious control. As a belief, I–E is learned, and as a belief, it is subject to change. It may not be easy, but I–E can change as our circumstances change, as our beliefs about ourselves change.

When we view I–E in this way it comes as no surprise to learn that women in many cultures tend to be more external than men do[5] – to be more likely to believe that luck, chance and powerful others control their lives. For women around the world it is a reality of life that action often does not produce the expected reaction, the expected outcome. Even with birth control there are unplanned pregnancies; even with competence and hard work, there is sex discrimination in the workplace; even in the face of legislation and trust, there is physical and sexual abuse.

Nor is it surprising that women who live in situations traditionally experienced only by men – female business students and managers, for instance – do not differ from their male counterparts in personal power. Over the years I have had the opportunity to measure the I–E of hundreds of undergraduate students, MBAs and business and government managers, and have never found consistent sex differences in these groups. Occasionally in one group, men will score more internal than women; occasionally in another, women will be more internal than men, but in the 15 years I have been testing managers and business students, no consistent sex difference has emerged. This finding suggests that circumstance rather than sex determines personal power.

If the men and women who are attracted to management, trained in management and promoted into management do not differ in their perceptions about controlling their own environment, do they differ in their ability to actually exert such control? Do they differ in their ability to influence others? Do they differ in interpersonal power?

## Interpersonal power

Interpersonal power is the ability to influence others, 'the ability', in Paula Johnson's words, 'to get another person to do or to believe something he or she would not necessarily have done or believed spontaneously'.[2] With this definition we move power beyond the notion of a personal, idiosyncratic belief and into the realm of relationships. It is with our interpersonal power that we interact with the world. At this more macro level, power is more visible than it is at the level of personal power and other people are more able to detect and articulate its presence.

People exert interpersonal power primarily through the communication of their status. They can influence others *verbally* by the words they say, with an articulate argument or through the use of an assertive vocabulary. They can influence others *paraverbally*, by the way they talk: by tone of voice, the loudness or depth of their voices, or even with their ability to interrupt. Or they can influence others *nonverbally*, without words: with gestures, with body posture or with the use of personal space. Neither the influenced nor the influencer need be aware of the process in order for influence to be exerted, in order for interpersonal power to be exerted.

In Chapter 2, where we examined sex differences in more detail, we looked at some of the many ways in which males' and females' communication styles differ. We learned that women and men use a different language – that they employ different verbal communications – and that 'men's language' is considered to be more powerful than 'women's language'. We saw also that men and women tend to use different paraverbal communications – that men are more likely to exert interpersonal power by dominating mixed-sex interactions, for example. Finally, we learned that the nonverbal communications of men tend to parallel the nonverbal communications of powerful people, while women are more likely to communicate nonverbally as powerless people. For instance, women are more likely to sit and stand in circumspect 'ladylike' positions, while men are more likely to expand their space into the personal space of others.

It is not surprising, given these sex differences, that the interpersonal influence of women and men differs as well – that women do not fare as well as men do in attaining recognition, compensation and perks from their organisations. Women are paid less than men are, even in female-dominated occupations[6] and in top-level international management. They tend, also, to progress more slowly in their organisations even when they appear, by objective criteria, to be equal to their male counterparts.[7] Furthermore, female managers are granted less time off for training and education than men are.[8]

Among presidents and vice-presidents in American corporations, those whom we would assume to be among the most interpersonally powerful people in the world, women's salaries are 42 per cent of the salaries of their male counterparts.[9] Furthermore, women at the top are significantly less likely than men at the top to receive other organisational perks such as stock options and bonuses. In one study,[10] male senior corporate officers received an average of six such perks, whereas no female senior corporate officer received more than two.

These data are drawn primarily from studies of large corporations. Surely one would expect that there are pockets of our working society in which women and men experience interpersonal power equally – in unions, for example, or in their own small businesses. However, even in these areas a gap exists. Women are grossly underrepresented among union executives and are, in fact, rarely found in those positions unless the union represents a female-dominated occupation.[11] As for entrepreneurs, these women tend to receive less favourable treatment from their banks than men. Although there is one recent study showing that men and women are equally likely to be allowed funding by their lending institutions,[12] this is a rare and recent phenomenon and women are still more likely to be required to provide collateral for their loans.[13]

This lack of interpersonal power that women so commonly experience in the workplace is reinforced, for most women, when they return home at night. If interpersonal power is to be measured by the extent to which people can influence others to do work for them, then most men who live with women are, by definition, more interpersonally powerful than the women with whom they live. In virtually every country in the world, the female sex role holds women responsible for work in the home. Even in the minority of families in which men and women share equally in house and child-care, women are still given and seem to accept the primary *responsibility*.[14] As we saw in Chapter 3, these families are extremely rare.

So ingrained is our assumption that men will hold the interpersonal power in this realm of their existence that women are unlikely to notice, much less to complain, about an imbalance of interpersonal power in the home. In one study of married female professors,[15] for instance, many of these women acknowledged that they spent less time on their careers and more time on child-care and housework than did their husbands; yet they did not consider the division of labour in their homes to be inequitable.

Women's and men's relative positions of interpersonal power are reinforced at home by women's and men's relative positions of interpersonal power in the workplace and are reinforced in the workplace by their relative power positions at home. It is known, for example, that many family decisions are made on the basis of financial contribution – that the spouse who earns the lower salary is the spouse who is most likely to stay home with sick children, for instance.[16] Since women tend to earn less than their husbands their bargaining power is lower, and they are usually left with the lion's share of family responsibilities. By assuming greater home responsibilities a woman can place herself in a precarious organisational position, allowing her energy to be sapped and reinforcing the sex-role stereotype of the poorly committed female worker.[17]

On a one-to-one level, on the level at which managers must interact hundreds of times daily, men have a clear edge that is reinforced in their roles of husband and father as surely as it is reinforced in the workplace. This is a complex area of study, however, because of the difficulty in separating sex and organisational status. In a study of interpersonal empowerment strategies,[18] for instance, women were found to be more acquiescent than were men; yet when the researcher reanalysed her data, she found that job dependency was a better predictor of acquiescence than was sex. It seems that male and female managers who were in highly dependent positions tended to acquiesce easily. In this study women were more likely than men to occupy highly dependent managerial positions.

As we examine sex differences in interpersonal power, it is easy to become pessimistic about the managerial future of women. How can women possibly exert organisational power when their interpersonal power is lower than that of men? Ironically, the greatest hope for sex equality in the interpersonal power of female managers may lie in the area of organisational power.

## Organisational power

Rosabeth Moss Kanter defines power as 'the ability to get things done, to mobilize resources, to get and use whatever it is that a person needs for the goals he or she is attempting to meet'.[3] I have adopted this definition, not to define 'power' as Kanter has done but to define the third, most macro level of power in this analysis: organisational power.

For decades, women and men shared the belief that women made poor bosses – that women should never be placed in the position of mobilising organisational resources. It was considered socially acceptable to ridicule women who had attained organisational power or to say that one would 'never work for a woman'. As recently as Margaret Thatcher's election, in fact, people on the street were more than eager to tell reporters that they would never vote for a woman: not that they disapproved of the attitudes and policies of Margaret Thatcher, per se, but that they would never assist a woman in mobilising the resources of their country. Slowly, something is changing, and through the literature on managerial effectiveness we see a very different picture being drawn.

The area of managerial effectiveness[19] is the literature most closely related to organisational power, for it examines the extent to which male and female managers are able to and are perceived to 'get things done' in their organisations. After centuries of people assuming that women made poor managers, the literature on managerial effectiveness is beginning to show a definite edge for women. As early as 1983, the research indicated that female and male managers were evaluated by their subordinates as being equally effective.[20] In yet another study conducted during the same period, female managers were viewed by their immediate supervisors and by their peers as being more effective than their male counterparts.[21] This positive evaluation of women as managers is particularly strong among female MBA students[22] and among female managers.[23] In this latter study, in fact, female managers rated their female counterparts as being intelligent, more likeable, more successful and more able than male managers.

The discrepancy is an obvious one: when organisational power is defined as the ability to mobilise resources, women are beginning to generate greater organisational power than men in a world in which women's access to organisational resources[24] and interpersonal power is more limited than that of men. In the fairest and most rational of systems, today's top executives would recognise this discrepancy and many more women would be promoted into upper management with the tools to effect greater change. While we await this event, it might be interesting to review the paradoxes of power that have been discussed in this chapter and to examine some of the ways in which women have coped with these paradoxes.

# Women in management

The thesis of this chapter is a simple one that will provide no startling revelation for even the most naïve. The lack of women in management is an issue, not of education and training, but of power. Time, patience and women's self-improvement do not apper to be the solution. The solution, in fact, is similar to the problem: power.

Now, let us review the power scores of male and female managers. In personal power, in beliefs about control of one's own environment, there are no consistent sex differences among managers. In interpersonal power – the ability to influence others – there are large and many sex differences, with men enjoying greater influence than women in their homes and in their organisations. Finally, in the area of organisational power, in the ability to mobilise resources, it is beginning to appear that managerial women are perceived as being more effective than their male counterparts.

This recent research raises as many questions as it answers. Foremost among them is the question: 'If women are less interpersonally powerful than men are – if they are less able to influence others – how are they better able than men to mobilise resources?', or more simply, 'How can women be less influential than men, but equally or more effective?' Although I know of no clear answer to this question I find myself returning, when I consider it, to the concept of personal power – feeling in control of one's environment.

## Internal–external locus of control

Personal power or internal locus of control (I–E) is an important organisational concept because it is strongly related to organisational power. It is known, for instance, that internals are better than externals at negotiation[25] and at solving difficult job-related problems[26] and that their workers tend to be more satisfied than are the subordinates of externals.[27] Furthermore, within supportive organisational environments internals take more active roles in their career management than do externals and are more likely than externals to be promoted.[28] Thus people who feel in control of their own environment seem to be better at getting things done. People who feel powerful are powerful.

However, there are no consistent sex differences in locus of control (personal power) among managers and managerial students; therefore, if personal and organisational power are related, we would expect there to be no sex differences in organisational power. Yet women, the recent research suggests, are beginning to acquire greater organisational power. Perhaps for women, even moderate levels of locus of control may result in high levels of managerial effectiveness. It is also possible that there are no real sex differences in organisational power – that when more sophisticated studies separating sex and organisational status are undertaken we will find that personal power and organisational power are directly related for both women and men.

In any case, women's organisational effectiveness will, in the long run, undoubtedly increase their status, which will in turn increase their interpersonal power. As their interpersonal power increases women cannot fail to become even more organisationally effective, for the ability to mobilise resources is often dependent upon the ability to influence others. In the short run (and the short run, as predicted in *Breaking the Glass Ceiling*,[29] will span several decades), there are day-to-day inequities in interpersonal power to address. It is to these inequities that people usually refer when speaking of sex discrimination in the workplace. And women's techniques for coping with these inequities are of interest to us here.

## Denial of personal discrimination

Women learn to cope with discrimination in a variety of ways. One of these methods, which researchers are only beginning to address, has come to be known as 'the denial of personal discrimination'. There is strong evidence that women clearly recognise the fact of sex discrimination in the workplace but that they fail to see how they, personally, have experienced discrimination.[30] Against all evidence to the contrary, individual women tend to see themselves as being justly treated, even though they recognise that women in general are not.

How is this possible? It is possible because, as Canadian psychologist Mel Lerner[31] has demonstrated, people strive to perceive their world as a just and fair place. In order for the world to be just and fair women must compare their situation, not to the situation of men in comparable positions, but to the condition of other less fortunate women.[32]

The word 'denial' conjures up many negative connotations, for we tend to think of people in denial as people who are not exhibiting good mental health. To deny what others perceive to be reality is usually considered to be an ineffective coping strategy; however, it may have some advantages. Perhaps if they had accepted the reality of their own treatment in our society, women all over the world would have turned off their alarm clocks and gone back to sleep, rather than facing the overwhelming challenge of sex-role liberation; and, as unfair as it may seem, women's ability to disassociate themselves from their own personal problems may have made their cause more credible and their arguments more effective. By not attaching personal blame to men, individual women may have made the integration of women into the workplace a less bitter pill for men to swallow. By denying the reality of personal discrimination, women, at whatever price they have paid, may have created a new reality for us all.[33]

## Conclusion

Research and writing in the area of women in management has been classified as being of two types: person-centred and organisation-centred. The person-centred approach, it has been argued, tends to focus on blaming the victim, on placing the responsibility for organisational change squarely on the shoulders of women. The organisation-centred approach, on the other hand, would focus on organisational policy and strategy.[34] This chapter and, for the most part, this book, and the literature on women in management tend to take the person-centred approach, addressing those things that women and men do in order to gain and maintain power as managers. The organisation-centred approach has clearly received less attention than it deserves, perhaps because it is less gratifying and more difficult for researchers to address these macro issues of organisational restructuring and economic social change than it is for them to study the behaviours of women and men as they play their managerial roles with other women and men. Few organisations but many individual men and women have contributed greatly to change; few organisations but many individual people seek information to effect change. Yet, however new and underdeveloped the field of women and management, it is beginning to tackle the big issue – 'the "genderness" of organizational management practices and conditions'[35] – the issue of power.

## Notes and References

1. This chapter appeared in an earlier form in Long, Bonita C. and Kahn, Sharon E. (eds), *Women, Work, and Coping*, McGill-Queen's University Press, Montreal & Kingston, London, Buffalo, 1993.

2. Johnson, Paula, 'Women and power: Toward a theory of effectiveness', *Journal of Social Issues*, vol. 32, no. 3, 1976, pp. 99–110.
3. Moss Kanter, Rosabeth, *Men and Women of the Corporation*, Basic Books, New York, 1977.
4. Rotter, Julian, 'Generalized expectancies for internal vs. external control of reinforcement', *Psychological Monographs*, vol. 80, 1966, pp. 1–28.
5. Lefcourt, H. M., 'Locus of control' In J. P. Robinson, P. R. Shaver and L. S. Wrightsman, (eds), *Measures of Personality and Social Psychological Attitudes: Volume 1 of Measures of Social Psychological Attitudes*, Academic Press, New York, 1982, pp. 413–99.
6. Abella, Judge R. S. *Equality in Employment: A Royal Commission Report*, Supply and Services Canada, Ottawa, 1984.
7. Egan, Mary Lou and Bendick Jr, Marc, 'International business careers in the United States: Salaries, advancement and male–female differences', *International Journal of Human Resource Management*, vol. 5, no. 1, 1994, pp. 33–50.
8. Cahoon, A. R. and Rowney, J. I. A. 'Variables influencing job satisfaction and stress in female managers', Paper presented at the meeting of the Canadian Psychological Association, Ottawa, June, 1984.
9. Nelson, S. and Berney, K., 'Women: The second wave', *Nation's Business*, May 1987, pp. 18–27.
10. Kosinar, S., 'Socialization and self-esteem: Women in management' In B. L. Forisha and B. H. Goldman (eds), *Outsiders on the Inside*, Prentice Hall, Englewood Cliffs, NJ, 1981, pp. 31–41.
11. Chaison, G. N. and Andrappan, P., 'Characteristics of female union officers in Canada', *Industrial Relations*, vol. 37, 1982, pp. 765–78.
12. Butner, H. and Rosen, B., 'Funding new business ventures: Are decision makers biased against women entrepreneurs?' *Journal of Business Venturing*, vol. 4, 1989, pp. 249–61.
13. Swift, C. and Riding, A., 'Giving credit where it's due: Women business owners and Canadian financial institutions', Paper presented at the International Council for Small Business Meeting, Helsinki, Finland, 1988.
14. Bem, Daryl, 'A consumer's guide to dual-career marriages', *ILR Report*, vol. 25, no. 1, 1987, pp. 10–12.
15. Yogev, S., 'Do professional women have egalitarian marital relationships?' *Journal of Marriage and the Family*, vol. 43, 1981, pp. 865–71.
16. Friedman, D. E., 'The invisible barrier to women in business', *Inside Guide*, vol. 2, 1988, pp. 75–9.
17. Blau, F. D. 'Occupational segregation and labour market discrimination' in B. F. Reskin (ed.), *Sex Segregation in the Workplace: Trends, Explanations, Remedies*, National Academy Press, Washington, DC, 1984, pp. 117–43.
18. Mainiero, L. A., 'Coping with powerlessness: The relationship of gender and job dependency to empowerment-strategy usage', *Administrative Science Quarterly*, vol. 31, 1986, pp. 633–53.
19. Dipboye, R. L., 'Problems and progress of women in management' in K. S. Koziara, M. H. Moskow and L. D. Tanner (eds), *Working Women: Past, Present, Future*, Industrial Relations Research Association Series, the Bureau of National Affairs, Washington, DC, 1987, pp. 118–53.
20. Terborg, J. R. and Shingledecker, P., 'Employee reactions to supervision and

work evaluation as a function of subordinate and manager sex', *Sex Roles*, vol. 9, 1983, pp. 813–24.

21. Tsui, A. S. and Gutek, B. A., 'A role set analysis of gender differences in performance, affective relationships, and career success of industrial middle managers', *Academy of Management Journal*, vol. 27, 1984, pp. 619–35.

22. Mickalachki, Dorothy M. and Mickalachki, Alexander, 'MBA women: The new pioneers', *Business Quarterly*, vol. 49, 1984, pp. 110–15.

23. Jabes, J., 'Casual attributions and sex-role stereotypes in the perceptions of female managers', *Canadian Journal of Behavioural Science*, vol. 12, 1980, pp. 52–63.

24. Stewart, L. and Gudykunst, W., 'Differential factors influencing the hierarchical level and number of promotions of males and females within an organization', *Academy of Management Journal*, vol. 97, 1982, pp. 586–97.

25. Stolte, J. F., 'Self-efficacy: Sources and consequences in negotiation networks', *Journal of Social Psychology*, vol. 119, no. 1, 1982, pp. 69–75.

26. Brousseau, K. R., 'Job–person dynamics and career development' in K. M. Rowland and G. R. Ferris (eds), *Research in Personal and Human Resources Management*, vol. 2, JAI, Greenwich, 1984.

27. Johnson, A. L., Lathans, F. and Hennesey, H. W., 'The role of locus of control in leader influence behaviour', *Personnel Psychology*, vol. 37, 1984, pp. 61–75.

28. Hammer, T. H. and Vardi, Y., 'Locus of control and career self-management among nonsupervisory employees in industrial settings', *Journal of Vocational Behaviour*, vol. 18, no. 1, 1981, pp. 13–29.

29. Morrison, A., White, R. and Van Velsor, E., *Breaking the Glass Ceiling*, Addison Wesley, Reading, Mass, 1987.

30. Crosby, Faye, 'The denial of personal discrimination', *American Behavioural Scientist*, vol. 27, no. 3, 1984, pp. 371–87.

31. Lerner, Melvin J., 'Just world research and the attribution process: Looking back and ahead', *Psychological Bulletin*, vol. 85, no. 5, 1978, pp. 1030–51.

32. Abbondanza, M., 'Cognitive barriers to intergroup equality between the sexes', Paper presented at the Meeting of the Canadian Psychological Association. Winnipeg, June 1983.

33. This section on denial of personal discrimination is lifted, almost verbatim, from Colwill, Nina L., 'Why does the phenomenon of women's denial of personal discrimination exist?' *Women in Management*, vol. 3, no. 1, 1992, pp. 4–5.

34. Fagenson, E., 'On women in management research methodology: Your theory is showing', Proceedings, Women in Management Research Symposium, Mount Saint Vincent University, Halifax, April, 1988.

35. Calas, M. and Smirchich, L., 'Using the "F" word: Feminist theories and the social consequences of organisational research', Proceedings of the Academy of Management, Washington, DC, August, 1989.

# 5

# Managers and Secretaries

## Susan Vinnicombe and Nina L. Colwill

In a relationship of fealty, then, secretaries were expected to be
bound by ties of personal loyalty, to value non-utilitarian
rewards, and to be available as an emotional partner. The image
of what secretaries wanted – and, by extension, working women
– was shaped by these expectations.

Rosabeth Moss Kanter

There are two sex-related issues in today's organisations that we believe
are intertwined: more than 95 per cent of secretaries in North America and
Western Europe are female; and more than 95 per cent of senior managers
in North America and Western Europe are male. What is the relationship
between these two statistics? Both derive from the belief that women, the
things that women do, and all things feminine are inferior to men, the
things that men do and all things masculine.

As members of a sex-role-liberated society, we try to provide male and
female managers with sex-neutral business education, equal opportunity
legislation and common workplace socialisation. Despite this goal, organisations continue to demonstrate a fundamental lack of recognition and
respect for female talents. Hence the secretarial role, populated primarily
by women, is characterised by low status, poor salary and dead ends; while
the management role, primarily populated by men, is characterised by
high status, attractive salary packages and achievement.

The bulk of our knowledge about women and work is based on the
study of women in business and management. This is not to argue that
researchers should abandon their projects on women in management or
that management should stop addressing the unique problems of their
female managers. Rather we need to expand our knowledge of sex-role

problems at work, for the study of women in management tells us only about the attitudes towards women who enter the male-dominated field of leadership, and discrimination against these women is only a manifestation of a much broader phenomenon: the devaluation of women and the work that women do.

Discrimination against women has made it necessary over the years for governments to encourage and to require organisations to recruit on the basis of qualifications, and to pay and promote on the basis of skills and experience. Government interference has been a catalyst that has benefited women in male-dominated occupations, allowing them the opportunity for their work to be measured by the same yardsticks as men's. Only recently have governments addressed the sub-issue – the devaluation of the work that women have traditionally done – with the implementation of 'comparable worth' legislation. The world of women and work has changed for the better over the last two decades, but until we address the problems faced by a larger cross-section of female workers, we will make little impact on the changes required. In order to appreciate fully why there are so few female senior managers, we need to know why there are so many female secretaries. We need to understand their job descriptions, their attitudes, the attitudes of their male and female peers and managers, their opportunities for promotion and the organisational structures in which they operate. Sex roles and work roles are intricate, multifaceted and ever-evolving, and we cannot hope to comprehend their complexities by focusing all our attention on the women who most closely resemble ourselves. Thus this chapter is devoted to secretaries.

## Growth of white collar work[1]

Although the position of the secretary is commonly observed in most organisations, there has been little systematic attempt to understand it. Secretaries rarely appear on organisation charts and frequently work beyond their job descriptions. This traditional lack of formal recognition clearly does not reflect the reality of the role of the secretary in managerial life. The extent to which organisations need secretaries becomes strikingly evident when they are unexpectedly absent and their hidden contributions suddenly surface. Put more cynically, organisations provide their managers with secretaries, as they do cars, yet more time is spent scrutinising and analysing the purchase, allocation, maintenance and expense of cars than is spent on considerations of the function, selection, performance and development of secretaries.

The enormous expansion of office jobs in the whole occupational spectrum must constitute one of the overriding characteristics of modern industrial societies. It is extremely difficult to define white collar workers along any single dimension of stratification. The features that are normally associated with them – type of dress, the nature of the work environment and the functions performed – can all be regarded as different external systems of a more fundamental common feature: the possession of or proximity to authority. Thus, although most white collar employees occupy subordinate positions in the organisation in the same way that blue collar employees do, they are associated 'with the part of the reproduction process where authority is exercised and decisions taken.'[2] This description is particularly relevant to secretaries, since their role essentially derives from their bosses, the managers in the organisation, who hold positions of authority and are traditionally associated with the process of decision-making.

## The growth of bureaucracy

One of the major factors affecting the growth of white collar work was the rise of 'big business'. The term 'bureaucracy' has been used in a number of ways: as a large-scale organisation with specialised functions, as the administrative subsystem of an organisation, or merely as characteristic of an organisation's functioning. The typical characteristics of bureaucracy are:

1. Hierarchy of authority.
2. Division of labour.
3. Formal work procedures.
4. Extensive rules.
5. Limited authority of organisational position.
6. Differential rewards by organisational position.
7. Rational discipline.
8. Impersonal contact.
9. Administration separate from management/ownership.
10. Emphasis on written communication.

The last three characteristics are particularly important because it was the increased complexity of communication and coordination associated with large numbers of staff that led to the need for a substantive administrative component in organisations. The transferral of communication and coordination from management to clerical staff may be explained in terms of efficiency. It is less costly for managers to delegate such functions than it is for them to carry out these tasks themselves. Furthermore, the increasing professionalism of managers has led them to disparage the administrative activities necessitated by their jobs. These assumptions are currently being challenged actively.

Tracy,[3] however, is more cynical. He suggests that secretaries form a completely separate and distinct element in the organisational structure – a 'para-hierarchy' of administrative talent or a grouping of people in positions parallel to a hierarchy. Michael Korda[4] sees secretaries in a similar manner, referring to them as 'alternative management', and gives several vivid examples of how they can function effectively on behalf of their managers as sounding-boards for ideas and as barometers of the organisational climate. This would certainly explain the absence of secretaries from traditional organisational charts.

Further, Tracy posits that the survival of all organisations is largely due to secretaries who increasingly compensate for their bosses, in direct proportion to the bosses' position in the hierarchy. He calls this concept the 'Productive Para-hierarchy Principle': 'In order to survive a dominant hierarchy must create and maintain a para-hierarchy composed of members of a subordinate class . . .'[3]

## From master of scrolls to office wife

The secretarial job has a long history. The word 'secretary' derives from the Latin *secretum*. In medieval times a secretary was the person who dealt with the correspondence of the king or other high-ranking person and, consequently, with confidential and secret matters. Although a variety of tasks are associated with the secretary today, the original notions of confidentiality and skill in correspondence are still the elements most traditionally linked with the occupation.

The introduction of the typewriter in 1875 in Great Britain marked the advent of women's entry into the office. One hundred years later, a standard female hierarchy has evolved in offices. At one end are the central word processor operators. These people usually work in a room with other word processing operators and their work consists wholly of copy typing that has been given to them by a number of managers or allocated to them by their supervisor. Their jobs are routine, with immediate visible results that are easily measured. Because success is entirely dependent on the speed and accuracy of their typing, communication with other people is not only unimportant but, in most cases, is disruptive to performance.

In her book *Men and Women of the Corporation*, Rosabeth Moss Kanter[5] relates the female private secretary to her male boss through the concept of the office wife, whose duty is to 'identify herself completely with her employer's interest and minister to his comforts and peace of mind'. The metaphor of the 'office wife' is apt, since the private secretary emerges as the boss's primary partner, support and confidante in the work context, much as does a wife in the home environment. In fact, it is not unknown for a private secretary to be more in touch with the boss's activities, both on a work and private front, than is his wife:

> . . . expectations of personal loyalty and symbolic or emotional rewards – and an emotional division of labour in which the woman plays the emotional role and the man the providing role. Indeed, the progression from the secretarial pool and multiple bosses to a position working for just one manager resembles the progressing from dating to marriage.

# Secretaries today

## The pink collar ghetto

The importance of identifying the sexist side of the secretarial role is important, because just as the majority of secretaries are female, so the majority of their bosses are male. A recent survey of 540 secretaries in the United Kingdom[6] demonstrated that their profile is young and female. Less than a quarter of the secretarial/administrative/clerical staff were older than 40 and around a quarter were male. (In studies in which secretaries alone are considered, the percentage of males is much lower.) Furthermore, 8 per cent of managers said that they would not employ a male secretary and 13 per cent were unsure if they would.

Low pay typifies the secretarial profession. Nearly a half (44 per cent) of the organisations surveyed gave their secretaries and administrators salaries below the low pay thresholds defined by the Low Pay Unit (£10,259) and the Council of Europe Basic Decency Threshold (£10,770). The report concludes that the pay levels are 'a clear measure of the low value that an organisation places on these staff'. Nearly two-thirds (64 per cent) of the secretaries surveyed were dissatisifed with their jobs: 39 per cent wanted to move into management and 25 per cent hoped to enter a completely different field. Only 11 per cent said that they were content to remain at their current level, and 14 per cent hoped to progress as a secretary.

The primary source of dissatisfaction for secretaries was related to poor career opportunities. Organisations spent less than 10 per cent of their training budgets on administrative and secretarial staff and secretarial work did not figure in graduate training programmes: yet in spite of this neglect, 38 per cent of secretaries believed that their organisations would promote them into management, although the survey uncovered few examples of such promotions. Catherine Truss and colleagues, in their recent research of secretaries in Publishing and Management Consultancy in England, France, and Germany, support the Industrial Society's survey. Just 21 per cent of the secretaries in her study felt that prospects for promotion within secretarial work were 'good' or 'excellent'.[7]

The English secretaries appeared to be much more optimistic about promotion opportunities. However, it seems that age is linked to attitudes to promotion and the English secretaries in this sample were younger than the French and German secretaries. Younger secretaries viewed their opportunities for promotion less negatively than older secretaries: 49 per cent of under 25-year-olds believed that their chances of promotion were 'bad' or 'none' compared with 80 per cent of those aged 46 or older. The Industrial Society concludes its 1994 report on secretaries by saying that managers' ageist and sexist attitudes have created for secretaries 'something of a "pink collar ghetto" characterised by low pay, lack of career development and skill wastage'.[6]

In an interesting study in 1990 23 female secretaries working for female bosses at a prestigious women's academic institution were interviewed. Each was asked about a variety of aspects of her work situation. Despite the many negative aspects inherent in the secretaries' descriptions of their jobs (for example, low pay and lack of opportunity for promotion, lack of prestige and challenge, limited decision-making power) the majority of them were positively disposed towards their overall work experiences. The secretary–boss relationship was characterised by cooperation, communication, support and mutual respect. The secretaries liked and admired their bosses, partly because they exhibited both sensitivity and competence–characteristics of a successful manager.[8]

## Personal characteristics of secretaries

Why do women continue to choose secretarial work? In 1981, Silverstone and Towler[9] administered questionnaires to 200 British secretaries and compared their answers to the responses of 500 secretaries sampled in 1970. In the 1970 group, 44 per cent said that they chose secretarial work because they were 'unable to do what they really wanted or could not think of anything else to do'. In the 1981 sample, only 19 per cent cited this reason. Instead, approximately a half said that 'good pay' had been an important factor, and that they expected a 'plentiful supply of jobs' and interesting work. A higher proportion of the 1981 sample (33 per cent), as compared to the 1970 sample (24 per cent), thought that secretarial work would offer a stepping stone into other types of employment. However, 60 per cent of the sample reported that they had no opportunity for promotion in their present jobs. A more recent survey of 5736 secretaries in the United States[10] indicates that 76 per cent of secretaries do not want their children to follow their career paths and 65 per cent of them think about leaving their jobs.

A study that compared male and female clerical–secretarial workers in a public sector institution[11] found that only 7 per cent of the workforce was male and that they were concentrated in clerical as opposed to secretarial posts. Men were found to be less committed to the occupation than were women and perceived a greater sense of occupational choice. Women tended to find the work more personally meaningful than did men. However, both sexes were extremely discontented with their developmental and promotional opportunities. Younger workers felt this gap in opportunity even more strongly than did older workers.

Two key observations emerge from these studies, which span the last two decades. Women are becoming more discriminating about choosing secretarial work, a fact that is worrying to managers since it is leading to a shortage of secretaries. Secondly, although it is overwhelmingly women who are attracted into secretarial/clerical work, both women and men are equally frustrated with the lack of job satisfaction and opportunities provided.

Given the problems facing today's secretaries, who are the women who choose secretarial work? In 1988, Teresa Sztaba and Nina Colwill[12] investigated the ways in which female students in secretarial work differed from female students in a male-dominated management degree programme. One of the measures they used in this study was the Personal Attributes Questionnaire (PAQ), a popular measure of masculinity and femininity. In the PAQ, described in more detail in Chapter 6, one attains a femininity score by describing oneself with stereotypically female characteristics such as 'very gentle' and one attains a masculinity score by describing oneself with stereotypically male characteristics such as 'very competitive'. The two sets of students differed from each other in several significant ways: the female secretarial students were more likely to be 'feminine' than were the female management students, who were more likely to be 'masculine'. The female students also differed on two of the three dimensions of the Locus of Control scale, a measure of personal power as described in Chapter 4. Secretarial and management students were equally likely to believe that they determined their own destiny. However, secretarial students were more likely than were management students to believe that luck or other powerful people determined their destiny. The expectation that powerful people will influence one's success or failure may be intimately related to a reluctance to enter male-dominated occupations.

Interestingly, the two samples did not differ in their attitudes towards women. They also did not differ in their willingness to work hard and in their consideration of the unfavourable reactions of others to their personal achievements. However, management students were higher in two aspects of achievement motivation: mastery and competitiveness. Finally, the students differed in the reasons they reported for choosing their programme of studies. The female management students were more likely to make their choices based on the extrinsic characteristics of their chosen career, for example status and money. The female secretarial students were more likely to base their career choice on 'the desire to interact with and help others.'[12] Kentel and Gage[13] agree that women's choice of feminine occupations may be related to a socialisation process that emphasises that it is not feminine to covet money, status and power.

# Secretarial issues

## *The private secretary: work-horse and show-piece*

Private secretaries may spend little or no time typing, since they often have their own junior secretaries to whom such tasks can be delegated. Instead, most of their day is spent in a supportive administrative capacity carrying out a variety of tasks, from making the coffee to representing their bosses at meetings. Private secretaries work very closely with their bosses and, indeed, their successes depend mainly on maintaining this coordinated team approach. Private secretaries not only undertake anything required of them by their bosses but also, and importantly, initiate many work-based activities themselves.

Again, the effectiveness with which private secretaries initiate work depends on how well they know their bosses and how well they can anticipate the needs of their bosses. Often such secretaries have spent many years, in some cases a working lifetime, with one boss. They frequently pride themselves on being able to predict precisely their boss's reaction in any given situation. It is not surprising that they are often used as the boss's barometer in decision-making. Whereas in the situation of the word processor operator it is easy to control work and measure performance, with the personal secretary workloads are contingent on the boss's workloads, and performance is difficult to gauge as the outcome is not always immediate or quantifiable. Word processor operators may be very successful in carrying out their duties but may adopt a calculated interest in their work, for example, by adhering strictly to office hours. This would be a formula for failure for private secretaries who would never be successful if they were not prepared to work late. They have to let their work demands define their day.

One of the key contributions of secretaries is the way they operate as a system of cliques within and between formal lines of authority, thus easing the handling of issues that might have taken much longer had they gone through the regular channels of communication. The importance of the secretary is particularly pronounced when the boss works on assignments away from the office.

It is essential that the boss and secretary think, plan and act as a team. Just as the success of a doubles partnership in tennis depends critically on the ability of each player to anticipate the shots of the other, to complement each other's style and to synchronise their game, similarly the boss and secretary should work hard at developing their team strategy.

## Defining the job

These descriptions typify opposite ends on a continuum defining a secretary's position. Once an individual moves beyond the role of a word processor operator it becomes difficult to define the job accurately, as it tends to be a blend of activities. The relative proportions that make up any one secretary's job are primarily determined by the boss, with the secretary bringing a certain amount of influence to bear. The nature of the boss's position and the industry in which it is located will also affect this situation.

Between the private secretary and the word processor operator are the departmental or group secretaries. Rather than working exclusively for one boss they tend to work for a group of managers. Thus they are unable to build the same degree of personal identification with their bosses as do private secretaries, and they are likely to undertake fewer administrative duties.

This particular secretarial arrangement has increased tremendously in the past few years, due to top management's belief that secretaries can work much faster with new technology. Group secretaries experience a number of work problems in trying to provide an efficient service to their bosses. They do not have the time to read all the paperwork that passes by them, they often suffer from innumerable interruptions, they are constantly juggling priorities and they invariably have little time to coordinate properly with all their bosses.

## Just a secretary

These pressures make many group secretaries feel over-stressed and frustrated at not being able to devote sufficient time to each work assignment. None of this is helped by the secretary's group of bosses who, instead of operating as a coordinated team, compete with one another for the secretary's time by completely ignoring each others' work demands.

When it comes to performance appraisal group secretaries count themselves lucky if they get one, and when they do, it is often conducted by one manager completely in isolation of the other managers in the group. It is no wonder that many group secretaries feel that their work goes unrecognised and is undervalued. A recent study in the United States indicated that employers still do not evaluate their secretaries' performance regularly and that their employers did not warn them of inadequacies before firing them.[14]

It is possible to reach the top secretarial positions in an organisation at a very young age. It does not follow, however, that promotion comes quickly or easily. Initially, promotion for a secretary is almost completely dependent on individual members of the managerial hierarchy spotting potential in the central pool or department. The individual then becomes a private secretary and further promotion up the organisational ladder usually depends upon the boss's promotion – a phenomenon called 'rug ranking'. In other words, bosses often carry their secretaries up the hierarchy with them. The reverse of this phenomenon is that many senior secretaries automatically lose their positions when their bosses are made redundant or fired. These secretaries must resort to picking up whatever secretarial roles are vacant in the organisation.

Similarly, the organisational criteria that are used to allocate private secretaries to their managers are irrational. When managers reach a certain level in the organisation, usually as a senior manager, they are automatically given a secretary. In this respect private secretaries operate as symbols of success and prestige for their respective managers. Thus, private secretaries are often perceived as perks or rewards for managerial performance rather than as individuals who are evaluated for their own work contributions.

## Patrimony lives on

The almost exclusively female nature of the secretarial position in the western world and the nature of a secretary's promotion through the organisation reinforces the appropriateness of the reference to the secretary as the office wife. Like the boss's wife, who may assume her social status through her husband, so do secretaries acquire their position and status through their bosses. Given the lack of standard job descriptions, rational criteria or performance appraisal schemes, secretaries are often in a relatively powerless position to manipulate their careers. According to a survey conducted by N.E. Fried and Associates, the percentage of organisations that use 'rug ranking' has fortunately dropped from 47 per cent in 1988 to 29 per cent in 1993.[15]

There is precious little incentive for managers to develop their secretaries. Managers are highly dependent upon secretaries who have learned to cater to their idiosyncrasies. The loyalty that the manager so often extracts from the relationship allows for the development of the secretary, but it is the development of a unique set of skills and knowledge that make the secretary the specialised support of one particular person. It is thus paradoxical that while the secretarial position was created through the bureaucratisation of organisations, it contradicts the principles of bureaucracy rationality, depersonalisation of relationships and the application of universal standards. The boss–secretary relationship represents the most striking example of the retention of patrimony.

In this respect it is a shame that organisations, if they train secretaries at all, persist in training managers and secretaries separately. Even in obvious areas such as time management, secretaries are often not incorporated into the management training programme. These practices undermine the role of the secretary in the office. Managers need to recognise that of all the resources available to them none are more critical than their secretaries.

## The new technology

New technology is also forcing a redefinition of roles and attitudes in relation to secretaries. A survey of top secretaries across Europe conducted through Management Centre Europe in the late 1980s highlighted some optimistic results. The impact of new technology was measured on five aspects of secretaries' jobs: job content, structure of the job, health and safety, work environment and work effectiveness. In no case did the secretaries feel that new technology had an overall negative effect. On the contrary, secretaries felt that it had significantly increased their job knowledge, skills and challenge and their working conditions. Of greater importance to management, secretaries reported that the most favourable responses they had to new technology were in the area of increased work effectiveness – quantity, quality and efficiency.

New technology has clearly revitalised many secretarial jobs. Where this has happened it appears to be linked to managers' positive attitudes towards their secretaries. They have actively involved them in planning and implementing the new technology and applying it to their jobs. On the other hand, if managers do not involve secretaries in introducing new technology and retain rigid attitudes about the manager's tasks and the secretary's tasks, then the secretary will not benefit from new technology. The secretary's job may well deteriorate into a permanently routine typing job, working for an increasing number of managers.

# The future of the secretarial role

The secretarial role is changing. Some say that the secretarial role is outdated and that it will disappear.[16] Increased office automation, commercial pressure and the decreasing supply of good secretaries will accelerate this situation. Managers will become fully computer-literate and will send and receive all their information themselves. Tom Peters[17] goes further. In one of his recent video cases . . .Opticon has made a concerted effort to cut out paper completely from the organisation. Any important ideas that need to be filed are entered straight onto the computer. Some secretaries have been transferred to personnel or public relations departments where their skills can be better harnessed.

Recent studies, however, have suggested an opposite trend. Twenty-four per cent of a Pitman survey[18] of personnel managers and directors expected the role of personal assistant to become more rather than less important. In a Canadian study[19] both managers and secretaries believed that the secretarial role is moving towards that of a paraprofessional – a situation in which there will be more administrative assistants and fewer secretaries. Skills expected to be important in this new role are broad: financial, organisational, training and decision-making and skills in languages, desk-top publishing, budgeting, policy interpretation, computer maintenance, facility logistics, graphic design and planning. In a 1990 survey conducted at the Professional Secretaries International Convention,[20] 75 per cent of the secretaries reported that they participated in decisions affecting their departments, 41 per cent in divisional decisions and 31 per cent in decisions affecting the company as a whole. Nearly half of the secretaries supervised other staff and 40 per cent controlled part of the budget.

> The role of the secretary is becoming less of a servant role to the manager and more of an administrative manager. Partnerships are beginning to form that are much more equal. If secretaries push this in the right direction – and many of them are – it could become an increasingly prestigious job within the company.

Tips for managers who want to benefit from the secretary's changing role include the following:

1. Make sure the support staff understands company and team goals.
2. Find out about the experience and skills of support staff members.
3. Ask the support staff for ideas.[21]

## Seven remedies against the crisis[22]

To remedy the impending secretarial crisis a strategy must be developed by all organisations that employ secretaries to improve their working lives. This strategy is built on the following seven key areas.

### 1. Job descriptions
In many organisations there are few attempts at job analysis of secretarial work. There is a pressing need to carry out a proper job analysis so that job descriptions can be drawn up and a grading structure established, based on job content rather than on the status of the boss. Job analysis could also be used as a vehicle for understanding how to enhance secretarial jobs.

### 2. Recruitment
If job descriptions were established, person specifications could be derived for any particular vacancy. Person specifications would help to focus the interviewing process on matching the person to the job instead of to the boss's vision of an ideal secretary.

### 3. Salary
At present the salary of the secretary is linked to the title or status of the boss, rather than performance. Once job descriptions have been established and the value of the job identified, then salaries can be linked accordingly.

### 4. Performance appraisal
Once a salary range for each position has been set, salary increases should be based upon merit. Each secretary should be evaluated based on the performance of tasks described in the job description and the objectives set at the previous performance appraisal interview. The systematic setting of performance standards of secretaries should help managers to recognise the value of their secretaries.

### 5. Team building
Managers must work closely with their secretaries on a day-to-day basis, keeping them well informed, and on a long-term basis, planning and developing work activities and helping them to understand how the whole organisation is performing. Secretaries need to be involved in all aspects of the boss's job – visiting other parts of the business, informal talks and group meetings. Secretaries have frequently been recognised as key organisational 'gate keepers' for their bosses. The recent wave of energy for empowering all employees in an organisation certainly needs to extend to secretaries.

*6. Career development*
If managers develop close, supportive work relationships with their secretaries, then they should also become involved in counselling them on their work and career development. The secretarial position is an ideal training ground for management. The new office technology may well spawn a new kind of office hierarchy, which brings together all the disparate office services such as data-processing, mail, telecommunications and printing, along with typewriting. If this occurs, a job in a word processing centre could well be a launching pad to a technical career, resulting in new and exciting changes for the incumbent.

*7. Training and personal development*
Secretaries should not be overlooked in the management training and development area. Most of them are eager to learn more and become more involved in the organisation. Moreover, research has shown that while women tend to choose male-dominated fields for extrinsic reasons such as status and money, they are more likely to choose female-dominated fields for their emphasis on interpersonal skills and service.[23] In the Total Quality Management culture of the 1990s which prizes people skills and service, surely secretaries must be an untapped pool of talent in many organisations. Management need to broaden its management development programmes in order to encompass secretaries. Secretaries need to be made aware that there are many traditionally masculine jobs through which they can use their people skills and keen sense of service.

# Conclusion

Implementation of this seven-point strategy will elevate the secretarial role to the position it has long deserved in organisations. New developments in office technology are proving to be the catalyst for organisational change. It is now up to senior managers to act as change masters in making it happen.

# Notes and References

1. Parts of the first two sections of this chapter have been summarised from Vinnicombe, Susan, 'The development of secretarial role', *Secretaries, Management and Organisations*, Heinemann, London, 1982.
2. Bain, G. S. and Price, R., 'Who is a white collar employee?' *British Journal of Industrial Relations*, vol. X, no. 30, 1972, pp. 325–39.

3. Tracy, L., 'Postscript to the Peter Principle', *Harvard Business Review*, July–August 1972.
4. Korda, Michael, *Power in the Office*, Weidenfeld and Nicolson, New York, 1976, pp. 83–5.
5. Moss Kanter, Rosabeth, *Men and Women of the Corporation*, Basic Books, New York, 1977.
6. 'Type Cast', *Industrial Society*, 1994.
7. Truss, Catherine, Goffee, Robert and Jones, Gareth, 'Career path in traditional women's jobs', *Women in Management Review*, vol. 7, no. 5, 1992, pp. 9–15.
8. O'Leary, V. E. and Ickovis, J. R., 'Women supporting women: Secretaries and their bosses' in H. Grossman and N. L. Chester (eds), *The Experience and Meaning of Work in Women's Lives*, Lawrence Erlbaum Associations, Hillsdale, NJ, 1990, pp. 35–56.
9. Silverstone, R. and Towler, R., 'Progression and tradition in the job of the secretary', Personnel Management, vol. 15, no. 5, 1983, pp. 30–3.
10. Anonymous, *Communication World*, vol. 10, no. 9, October, 1993, p. 9.
11. Hunt, Gerald, 'Sex differences in a pink-collar occupation', *Industrial Relations – Quebec*, vol. 48, no. 3, 1993, pp. 441–59.
12. Sztaba, Teresa and Colwill, Nina, 'Secretarial and management students: Attitudes, attributes and career choiuce considerations,' *Sex Roles*, vol. 19, nos. 9/10, 1988.
13. Kentel, W. F. and Gage, B. A., 'The restricted and gender-typed occupational aspirations of young women. Can they be modified?' *Family Relations*, vol. 32, 1983, pp. 129–38.
14. Wendt, Ann C. W. and Sloanaker, William M., 'Bosses and secretaries: Profiles of discrimination', *Review of Business*, vol. 14, no. 2, 1992, pp. 36–40.
15. N. E. Fried and Associates, 'Skills, not rugs, for rating secretaries', *Training*, vol. 30, no. 6, 1993, p. 14.
16. Carroll, Carol Ann, 'Secs change', *International Management*, vol. 48, no. 6, 1993, p. 52.
17. Peters, Tom, 'Management Revolution and Cororate Reinvention'. BBC Videos, London, 1993.
18. McHugh, Linda, 'The executive secretary in a changing world', *Executive Secretary*, vol. 4, no. 1, 1992, pp. 8–13.
19. Temple, Linda and Colwill, Nina L., 'The future of the secretarial role: The perceptions of secretaries and managers'. Paper presented at the ASAC Conference.
20. Forrest, Diane, 'From handmaiden to power behind the throne', *Canadian Business*, vol. 45, no. 6, 1991, pp. 48–53.
21. Jonson, Virginia, 'Changing Times: The evolving role of the secretary', *Successful Meetings*, vol. 40, no. 8, 1991, pp. 99–101.
22. This section is taken, almost verbatim, from the article by S. Vinnicombe and N. L. Colwill, 'Putting secretaries in their place: within the corporate strategy', *Management Centre*, Europe's International Management Development Review, 1988.
23. Strange, C. C. and Rea, J. S., 'Career choice considerations and sex role self-concept of male and female undergraduates in nontraditional majors', *Journal of Vocational Behavior*, vol. 23, 1983, pp. 219–26.

# 6

# Training, Mentoring and Networking

## Susan Vinnicombe and Nina L. Colwill

The first problem for all of us, men and women, is not to learn, but to unlearn.

Gloria Steinem

To this point the book has examined the position of women in European management and has sought to understand the situation by examining sex differences, the work–family interaction, power and powerlessness, and the relationship between the female-dominated secretarial position and male-dominated management. In this chapter it turns to solutions: training and development, mentors and protégés and networking.

## Training and development[1]

Five years ago one of the authors launched an elective on 'Women in Management' for the female MBA students at Cranfield School of Management. All the female students, who comprised 10 per cent of the class of 165, chose to take the elective; but their reactions were sharply divided. About half the women (the majority of whom were in their thirties) believed that the elective was an essential component of the MBA programme. They felt that it was needed to compensate for what they perceived to be an overly male-dominated experience. These women made four specific complaints about the MBA programme with regard to gender:

1. The faculty was comprised almost exclusively of men, who brought their conventional male attitudes and values into their teaching.

74

2. The materials were often sexist; it was difficult to find a case study with a female in a senior organisational position.

3. There was no opportunity to raise for discussion issues relating to women and work: e.g. sex-role stereotypes, attribution of success and failure, power and politics, dual-career families or sexual harassment.

4. Many of the management theories and principles being propounded in class were based on research with male managers exclusively.

David McClelland's seminal work on the need for achievement provides a good example. The results from his female samples were so 'confused' that he decided to throw them out and work exclusively with males. Similarly, Friedman and Rosenman's famous book, *Type A Behavior and Your Heart*, which is considered to be a classic in the area of stress, is based on a study of 3000 men.[2] (Type As are extremely competitive and hostile, attributing their successes to their ability to accomplish many things quickly.) Examples such as these call into question the application of these management research findings to women managers.

While half the female MBAs applauded the introduction of an elective to help them put into context their experiences of managerial life, the other half was sceptical about the elective. They resisted the idea that there are any issues attached to being a woman manager. Any problems they encountered at work, they believed, were equally applicable to male managers. They felt that working with an exclusive set of women managers on any kind of training event was dangerous, because it was contrived and because it had the potential to become a session in which participants simply cosseted their own values and behaviour through blaming men.

The Cranfield women MBA experience: (1) encapsulates the extreme views that exist on the subject of women-only training and (2) demonstrates that opposition to women-only training does not come only from men. Of course, not all work problems encountered by female managers can be reduced to the issue of sex. For this reason a women-only training programme is a critical part, but only a part, of a female manager's entire programme of management development. Women do share some special characteristics that make their experience of managerial life different to that of their male counterparts.

## The argument for women-only training

Life differs for the average man and the average woman in various ways, many of which exert a profound impact on their working lives and in their personal and family lives, as discussed in Chapter 3.

□ Women are more likely than men to have been absent from the work-place or to have worked part-time in the interest of children or family.

□ Women are more likely than men to accept the major share of the household and family responsibilities, placing an extra strain on their time, energy and areas of commitment.

□ Husbands are more likely than wives to be engaged in careers which, by virtue of their greater earning potential, take precedence over those of their partners, further widening the gap in their earning potential.

In their work lives:

□ Women are more likely than men to suffer from sex discrimination.

□ Women rarely have female role models in senior positions in their organisations. Further, the same women may have to serve as role models to more junior women, thereby increasing their stress.[3]

Many women in male-dominated fields feel that they are operating in an alien world in which the rules of power and politics require great investments of emotional energy to understand and to practise,[4] or that they are working alongside men who do not share or empathise with their values.[5]

Women's unique issues are rarely raised in mixed-sex groups, partly because of the fundamental differences between male and female communication patterns. As we saw in Chapter 2, men tend to dominate mixed-sex groups, to talk more and to make more suggestions than women; women spend more of their verbal time yielding, agreeing and praising others. Men initiate and are the recipients of the majority of verbal interactions. Men interrupt more than women and women are more likely to be the object of these interruptions. Furthermore, although men express their feelings more openly in mixed-sex groups, women express theirs more easily in all-female contexts. Taken together, these studies clearly indicate that women do not enjoy equal participation with men in any type of mixed-sex training.

Women may also be reluctant to discuss home and workplace conflicts with men, lest they be seen as incapable of coping.[5] Working through such conflicts is integral to women's psychological wellbeing. Women-only programmes are important because they encourage participants to talk about these experiences.

## The content of women-only training

Women-only training exists primarily because there are certain broad-based issues that can best be addressed in women-only groups, where women do not have to protect men's feelings. It is not surprising that, whether or not they are specifically written into the course outline, certain issues surface in most of these programmes: power and politics, sexuality, working styles, stress and career development.

## Organisational power and politics

The fundamental issue arising in most women-in-management courses is women's difficulty in handling organisational power and politics, as discussed in Chapter 4. For many women the focus at work is clearly on task accomplishment; they do not see the relevance of politics, or they may make actively disdain politics. It is important therefore to discuss with women managers the critical role of politics in organisations. To help women develop positive attitudes towards politics and political skills is the greatest challenge in these programmes. The advancement of women in management is contingent on women understanding how politics operate in their own organisations.

## The issue of sexuality

Sexuality is a workplace issue, and one that women often find easier to discuss among themselves. Is the office romance ever worth its attendant frustrations? How should one deal with a well-liked colleague who is becoming romantically involved? How does one deal with unwelcome sexual innuendoes from peers? How does one deal with a superior whom one suspects of being capable of sexual assault? These issues are difficult ones for women and men to discuss openly, because women and men are affected in fundamentally different ways: women form the great majority of victims in sexual harassment cases. The discussion of workplace sexuality is even more sensitive when the topic of sex and aggression arises. In recognition of the traumatic effects of sexual aggression on its employees Dupont has initiated a rape prevention programme, the core of which is an 8-hour women-only rape prevention workshop.[6]

## Sex differences in working styles

Research to support the idea of differences in the working styles of male and female managers is difficult to locate. The inappropriateness of the profiles used commonly in the leadership area to illuminate sex differences does not help this situation. However, research at Cranfield School of Management[7] using the Myers Briggs Type Indicator (MBTI), which is based on Jung's personality types, has yielded some significant and interesting findings about the differences between male and female working styles. The most significant difference between male and female managers is along the sensing/intuition dimension. Sensing people tend to prefer practical problems, systems and methods; are patient with routine details; and search for standard problem-solving approaches. Intuitive people enjoy ambiguous problems, get bored with routine problems, frequently ignore the facts and search for creative approaches. Women managers tend to be much more intuitive; 70 per cent of male managers in the Cranfield study were sensing, whereas 40–60 per cent of the women were intuitive depending on professional backgrounds. This is a positive finding, given that organisations require different kinds of management styles.

## Stress

The nature of women's stressors, the reasons behind their stress and women's responses to stress are different from those of men. Traditionally women have been socialised not to be aggressive or competitive, but to nurture. Braiker[8] identified that 'success' means something different to women and men. While men tend to define success in terms of quantifiable measures of achievement – money, status, material possessions – women tend to define success in terms of how well life is going in an emotional or interpersonal sense. While many men's success is primarily geared to achievement in the workplace, women's success is defined in terms of meeting a relentless stream of demands (often conflicting) from everyone around her at work and at home. Braiker[8] labels this stress syndrome the Type E:

Type E women often assume unrealistic and excessive burdens. They want to keep everyone's approval – that is part of how they know that they're succeeding and they cope with the demands by trying to do it all, often at a substantial cost to their emotional and physical well-being.

Because women do not express anger or aggression as easily as men, they may not even recognise their feelings as being anger. The anger may be disguised as resentment, depression or moodiness. Since most women's experiences of stress do not coincide with most men's experiences of stress, it is valuable to provide women with their own forum to discuss what stresses them, the consequences of their stresses and how they handle stress.

## Career development

Socialisation and upbringing often leave women focusing on the importance of caring for others rather than asserting themselves. This is an especially apparent factor in career development. Women often have difficulty in defining their careers, which is a great block to career progress. Women managers can help one another to see the themes in their careers, using a structured career exercise, such as Edgar Schein's Career Anchors.[9] The latter is particularly relevant to women because it defines the individual's self-image (abilities and talents; motives and drives; and attitudes and values) through analysing all her varied work experiences. In so doing, the exercise helps women to integrate what many women see merely as a series of jobs and to see future possible career choices.

Edgar Schein's Career Anchors exercise is additionally helpful to women managers, for not only does it pull together what women see only as 'a series of jobs', it also empowers women by showing them how they have influenced the shape of their careers to date. The importance of balancing career and family is often central to women. The career anchors exercise highlights this orientation.

# The design of women in management programmes

Women in management programmes are basically of two types, both of which we discuss in this chapter. There are those that address general management topics such as accounting, marketing and strategy; there are those, such as the University of New Brunswick's women-only mini-MBA-type programme, for example, that address general management topics such as accounting, marketing and strategy. There are others, such as Cranfield School of Management's personal development programme for female managers, that primarily address the social–psychological issues facing women in the workplace.

In 1983 the University of Brunswick in Fredericton, Canada, launched a novel management development programme for women. Several years in preparation, this ten-month programme is aimed primarily at university-educated women who are currently employed and who wish to broaden their career prospects. Participants attend monthly three-day workshops in such areas as finance, marketing, organisational behaviour and business strategy. Each month they receive an assignment to be completed at their workplace, and each monthly session begins with a review of the previous month's assignments. Female academics from across Canada combined their expertise to design the programme, which is taught by female tutors with an interest in women's issues as well as in their own substantive areas. The participants are aspiring women managers from a variety of industries who are sponsored by their organisations. While the focus is on core management skills, the culture is one of shared personal issues and emotional support.

For the past eight years Cranfield School of Management has been running personal development programmes for women managers. In these programmes the female participants work with experienced female tutors in small groups, in an informal, highly interactive manner. The emphasis is on working through the personal issues facing the participants in their work and private lives and on the key attitudes that block their progress. Throughout, the aim is to be not only positive and constructive, but also confronting.

These women's programmes generally address the social–psychological issues facing women in the workplace. Participants undertake the following kinds of objectives:

1. To clarify their attitudes and feelings about themselves in relation to their work roles and personal roles (e.g. colleague, boss, wife, mother, daughter).

2. To review their experiences of managerial life: the specific issues they face as women and the resources they have at their disposal.

3. To examine their management styles, in order to promote their personal strengths at work.

4. To study the concepts of assertiveness and power and to enable themselves to apply these concepts effectively.

5. To help themselves to become more proactive in managing their careers.

6. To satisfy these goals in a safe environment in which they can test their own experiences against the experiences of other women.

Throughout the programmes the emphasis is on helping women managers to help themselves become more effective. Introducing participants to the concepts of role models, networking and mentoring are invaluable here. Perhaps most important of all is the support and friendship they are able to give to one another.

## Recommendations for women-only training

Having argued the need for women-only training and suggested some key topic areas to address in such training, the task still remains a challenge.

The following points might serve as a checklist for anyone thinking of establishing such a programme:

1. Because women's issues are often viewed as frivolous, women-only training can easily gain the reputation of the 'girls' day out'. Thus it must receive clearly articulated support from top management if it is to function as a credible in-house educational programme. Similarly, top-down support must be given to those attending the women-only training. It often helps if the training is run by authoritative external trainers.

2. Be prepared to face accusations of sex discrimination when instituting women-only training programmes and be prepared to offer male-facilitated male-only training in order to give interested men the opportunity to address sex-role issues in a safe environment as well. One might also consider combining men and women's groups at some point into a 'Men and Women Working Together' programme. If this latter format is utilised, it is imperative that both male and female facilitators be used and that they be able to serve as positive role models in their interactions with both sexes.

3. Ideally the programme should be offered in several modules, separated by weeks or months. Many of the issues that arise in women-only training are based on deeply rooted attitudes that require time to process, and many of the concepts may remain abstract until applied and internalised in the workplace.

4. It is important that women-only training be targeted to a specific group of women (for example, top-level managers or first-line supervisors) or address a specific issue, otherwise participants may find that they have nothing in common but their sex.

5. In organisations in which this training is being offered in-house, a decision must be made as to whether participants should be nominated according to set criteria or if they should be self-selected. The former method allows the organisers to create the relative homogeneity they desire, and may serve as effective organisational rewards. However, the same method may result in a less highly motivated group of participants and may engender resentment among those who were not selected. When the course is being offered by external agencies, the latter should be involved in deciding on the method of selection.

6. Residential workshops constitute an ideal learning environment. If child-care is an issue for participants, it is important to give serious consideration to the timing of the programme and to the possible provision of on-site day-care, in a way that suggests that home responsibilities are respected.

7. It is vital that the training draw to a positive conclusion. This goal requires a skilled facilitator with a positive view of life, one who is experienced in dealing with negative reactions and is not easily drawn into anger herself.

8. Ensure that none of the training materials are sexist in their assumptions or their language. Although it counteracts this non-sexist ideal, the group facilitator must be a woman.

9. Avoid an anti-male stance, if for no better reason than that it encourages the workshop to develop a female-victim/male-persecutor tone, a tone that is damaging to the self-concepts of the participants.

10. It is imperative that women-only training be seen as an adjunct to, rather than a substitute for, more traditional organisational and managerial training. Such training must be treated merely as one specific part of a comprehensive career development programme for female employees.

Of course, training programmes specifically designed for women in management do not provide the complete answer to the problems that women managers experience. To date, however, women have not only benefited from significant personal development but have also used the programmes as a springboard for further initiatives – particularly mentoring and networking. We now turn to these two important practices.

# Mentors and protégés[10]

The concept of mentoring has its origins in Greek mythology. Ulysses entrusted his son, Telemadus, to the care and direction of his friend, Mentor, while he went off to fight in the Trojan wars. The word 'mentor' has since become synonymous with wise counselling and has, in recent years, been adopted as a conscious development option by many companies.

In her book *The Change Masters*, Rosabeth Moss Kanter[11] has argued that all companies intent upon excellence should encourage managers to become mentors to their employees. In *Power and Influence*, John Kotter[12] agreed that mentors, sponsors, coaches and role models can be especially important in helping young people during their early careers. He said:

Virtually all the successful and effective executives I have known have had two or more of these kinds of relationships early in their careers.

Some have had upwards of a dozen people they were able to rely on for different needs – some provided important contacts, others gave key information in specific areas, and still others taught them certain valued skills.

From the point of view of organisational leaders, mentoring ensures 'the smooth transfer of the company culture between one generation of managers and the next', a process necessary 'for the long term corporate growth and survival of the company'. Learning 'how power is gained and wielded within a company' can only be transmitted through first-hand contacts with 'insiders'. When mentoring works well, the new junior manager 'will have detailed knowledge of how to handle both peers and subordinates' and will know 'how to exercise and feel comfortable with power'.[13]

The junior manager who is receiving mentoring is described as a 'protégé'. Mentoring is concerned with helping the learner through life crises or into new phases of development. The protégé receives active career sponsorship, the mentor gains 'a very useful ally' and the company benefits from 'rich, informal communication networks'.

The role of a mentor is difficult to define, for the function is informal and voluntary. Having a mentor is like having one's own career development officer. A mentor goes beyond the call of obligation into the realm of guardian angelship. A boss teaches a subordinate what to do, but a mentor presents a protégé with a privileged view of what to be. Mentors are surrogate parents, experts in subtle modelling, in well-placed introductions to people and ideas and, probably most important, in the subtle art of letting go.

The mentor is not normally the protégé's boss. Managers who, for whatever reason, are unsupportive of an individual subordinate can render the subordinate's career progression untenable. Even in the ideal situation the immediate boss is more concerned with meeting business targets than with meeting staff development needs, and the responsibility of the boss to evaluate the subordinate's performance will tend to block open communication. The mentor, on the other hand, could be compromised if asked to comment on the protégé's performance, and for this reason the mentor is usually not involved in the appraisal process.

The organisational reality of women and the organisational reality of men is never quite the same. Just as training needs can differ to a greater or lesser degree for male and female managers, so do the complex issues surrounding mentorship and its reciprocal, protégéship. In this section, we examine characteristics of the ideal mentor and protégé, explore potential problems in the male-mentor/female-protégé relationship. and ask the question: 'Who should mentor whom?'

## Ideal mentor and ideal protégé

In a study of *Business Quarterly* readers' attitudes toward mentorship,[14] 72 respondents rated themselves, their ideal mentor and their ideal protégé on the Personal Attributes Questionnaire (PAQ) – a popular measure of masculinity and feminity.[15] In the PAQ one attains a feminine score by describing oneself with such stereotypically female characteristics as 'very gentle'. A masculinity score is attained by describing onself with such stereotypical male traits as 'very competitive'. There were no sex differences in masculinity or femininity scores among the men and women who completed this questionnaire, nor were there any sex differences in their descriptions of their ideal mentor or their ideal protégé.

When asked if they would be more or less comfortable with a mentor and a protégé of their own sex, a bare majority of respondents said that it would make no difference to them. There were, however, sex differences among those who stated a preference. Men were more than twice as likely as women to state a sex preference for their ideal protégé and were 12 times as likely to prefer a male protégé. Men were twice as likely as women to express a sex preference for mentors and 25 times as likely to prefer a male mentor.

When asked to describe their ideal mentor and protégé, respondents did not describe people who were particularly masculine or particularly feminine; rather, they described people who had characteristics similar to those they had described in themselves. However, there were certain ways in which the ideal mentor and the ideal protégé differed from the respondent. These characteristics are outlined in Table 6.1.

Looking at the first five characteristics of ideal mentors and protégés, which are in fact shared, it seems that both women and men want a mentor and a protégé who is calmer and more predictable than themselves, as well as being amiable and independent. In addition, ideal mentors are probably best described as possessing leadership characteristics. The ideal protégé, on the other hand, would be devoted and would cry more easily than the respondent. This latter characteristic may indicate that the mentor feels needed by protégés who are prepared to share their feelings with them.

This research and the research of others suggests that similarity in the personal traits of mentors and protégés may play a more important role in their pairing than does the sex of the mentor and protégé. When given gender as the only variable with which to make a decision, women show little or no preference and men who have a preference prefer men. However, when asked to describe the characteristics of their ideal mentors and protégés, both men and women choose people who are similar to themselves rather than people who are stereotypically masculine or feminine. Whatever their choice, it is the reality of today's organisations,

**Table 6.1** Comparisons between self and ideal protegé and between self and ideal mentor.

| Compared to self, the protégé should: | Compared to self, the mentor should: |
| --- | --- |
| • Be less excitable in a major crisis<br>• Have feelings that are less easily hurt<br>• Be warmer in relations with others<br>• Be less emotional<br>• Have lower need for security<br>• Be more able to devote self to others<br>• Cry more easily | • Be less excitable in a major crisis<br>• Have feelings that are less easily hurt<br>• Be warmer in relations with others<br>• Be less emotional<br>• Have lower need for security<br>• Have less need of others' approval<br>• Be more active<br>• Be more aware of feelings of others<br>• Have less difficulty making decisions<br>• Be more confident<br>• Be able to stand up better under pressure<br>• Be more worldly |

in which men tend to occupy the top positions, that most male and female junior managers will be mentored by men. The male–male pairing is as ancient as work, but the male–female pairing was, until recently, a rare phenomenon and one that deserves some attention here.

## Male mentors and female protégés

Sex-role problems in organisations occur when our sex roles become more salient than our work roles and interfere with the smooth running of the organisation. In this section, we examine some of the ways that this can happen in the male-mentor/female-protégé relationship.

### Identifying with the protégé

The number of would-be protégés on the bottom looking up greatly exceeds the number of potential mentors on the top looking down. The demand for mentors to smooth the passage of people treading new organisational ground increases as more men and women enter occupations nontraditional for their sex. But these nontraditional people, the very ones who need the most guidance, may be those least likely to be chosen. Mentors tend to be attracted to their own kind and there are few top-level executives whose mirror reflects a woman. As one employee in a large corporation put it: 'Boy wonders rise under certain corporate structures. They're recognized by a powerful person because they're very much like him. He sees himself, a younger version, in that person. . . . Who can look at a woman and see themselves?'[16]

### Father–daughter relationship

Probably the greatest sex-role risk in male-mentor/female-protégé relationships is the risk inherent in father–daughter relationships: the risk of over-parenting. The female protégé cannot be Daddy's little girl. Like sons and male apprentices from time immemorial, she must be guided to independence. Sometimes that is a difficult task for the man who finds himself bombarded with messages from half a century of sex-role training – cues that seem to demand that this trusting young woman be pampered and protected. That is not the stuff of which strong managers are built, and just as over-parenting can stunt the growth of parents and children, so can it stunt the organisational and personal growth of mentors and protégés.

### Sexuality

The pairing of men and women into mentor–protégé relationships is a particularly easy target for accusations of sexual liaison, given the level of intimacy that the relationship naturally engenders. The research in this area indicates quite the opposite, however; men and women involved in this special pairing are highly unlikely to form sexual alliances. Perhaps their rarity forces them to live in an organisational fishbowl. Perhaps the pragmatic function of the relationship for both parties decrees that they operate with sexual blinders, lest the delicate balance be upset. Perhaps the father–daughter nature of the relationship establishes an incest taboo. Whatever the reason, sexuality appears to be the least of their sex-role problems.

### The assistant-to

Another trap in which male mentors and female protégés may find themselves ensnared is the reciprocal role of the overworked man and his female helpmate. Because men are accustomed to being assisted by women, it is easy to slip out of the mentor–protégé relationship and into the roles of 'busy manager' and 'assistant to the busy manager' – the power behind the throne. It is not that helpmates are not learning anything; they are simply not learning to be successors.

### The token protégé

Rosabeth Moss Kanter's[16] research points to yet another potential problem: executives may choose female protégés in order to demonstrate their ability to handle a tricky management situation or to provide themselves or their organisation with a show-piece. The woman may be an excellent performer or her performance may be barely adequate, but in either case she is a token protégé and the probability of her receiving the same treatment as her male counterpart is dismally low.

# Who should mentor whom?

The purpose of these cautions is not to discourage men from choosing female protégés and women from seeking the mentorship of highly placed men. In fact, it is only through mixed-sex mentoring that these problems will disappear. However, it does raise a question about which combination is the best: 'Who should mentor whom?'

It would be easy to argue that women should be mentored by women and men by men. This solution would certainly eliminate many sex-role problems in organisations. In addition, mentors would be dealing with protégés with whom they could easily empathise and protégés would be provided with same-sex role models with whom they could easily identify. In fact, it is usually assumed that the best possible mentor for every aspiring female is a more highly placed female.

There is an obvious flaw in this argument. Many organisations do not employ even one woman who could serve as a mentor and women who do occupy top-level positions would either have to ignore the talents of the majority of female candidates or devote their entire careers to mentorship. Women would be even less likely to be mentored than they are now.

The arguments against exclusive same-sex mentorship are no weaker from the overall view of the organisation. More than 30 years ago, Moore[17] warned the business community about the threat to organisational creativity inherent in a system of 'homosexual reproduction', in which the man in the grey flannel suit creates successors in his own image. Today we call that phenomenon cloning. If male executives choose their likenesses and coach them into even greater similarity, why would we suppose that female executives would be less diligent in choosing women who clearly resemble them and in moulding them into identical products? The result would be two corporate types: women and men. We would be widening the gap and increasing the conflict between the sexes.

Male-mentor/female-protégé relationships can be fraught with problems, to be sure, and there may be sex-role problems inherent in female-mentor/male protégé relationships that have yet to be discovered. Even as women can rarely find same-sex mentors, it will be a long time before men can be readily paired with female mentors, for women are not represented at the top in large numbers. As long as men continue to mentor young women, women can probably best speed equality by using at least some of their energy to mentor young men.

Someday gender will be an irrelevant issue in management. Until it is, and to speed the day, a broader view of mentorship, a wider vision of role modelling and the encouragement of cross-sex mentorship will provide men and women with new perspectives and provide their organisations with a more versatile and creative executive pool than ever before. Women at every organisational level can assist the process through networking.

# Networking[18]

Whenever a noun starts being used as a verb, the underlying concept can be safely assumed to be deeply entrenched in our society. So it is with networking, the banding together of like-minded people for the purposes of contact and friendship and support.

Networking in the context of women's networks – simply women's response to what has been called the 'old boy's network' – is women's attempts to create for themselves the support generated for men by their informal same-sex grouping. From this initial concept, three different types of women's networks have evolved[19] as follows:

1. *Professional and occupational networks* bring together women who have similar professional qualifications – Women in Engineering or Women in Management, for example – in order to provide information and career guidance. Through such groups women learn what is happening in their profession, their occupation or their industry. In 1984 the Brussels-based European Foundation for Management Development sponsored a cross-cultural network to address issues pertaining to women in business. A members' directory, a regular newsletter and an annual conference are three of the benefits of individual and institutional membership under the title European Women's Management Development Network.

2. *In-company networks* are formal or informal female groupings within a particular organisation. Some are open only to women at a particular organisational level – usually to women in management – and others address the shared concerns of all women in that organisation.

3. *Training networks* are women's support groups that grew out of women's training – a specific, general or professional training course. They are formed when women who have met for another purpose see themselves as being of like mind and decide that they would want to meet regularly to form an ongoing support group.

There is some evidence that networking serves a different function for men than it does for women: something more utilitarian and less social, perhaps. On the utilitarian side, it appears that male networkers are more likely than female networkers to call back favours from members of their network. In one British study, for example, 70 per cent of male senior executives, a percentage twice as high as that of these female counterparts, found their jobs through networking.[20]

Networking serves other, less instrumental functions, one of which is a socialising function, and the organisational social needs of women and men and the satisfaction of those needs appear to be quite different. In one study of Canadian accountants,[21] women considered lunching with their colleagues to be a more important social activity than did men; they engaged in it significantly more (182 times a year) than did men (152 times a year); and they considered it to be significantly more stress-reducing than did men. As the researchers said:

> Lunch can provide an affiliating function, an information-gathering function, and a socialisation function for both women and men. It appears, however, that for women in particular, it is a critical component of the work day. In organisations in which women are being integrated into professional and management roles, supervisors would be wise to encourage this interaction among their male and female subordinates.

There are other ways in which women and men experience the workplace differently. Although women may place great importance on the socialising aspect of networking, they tend to be excluded from many of the social events and workplace conversations in which men engage. Looking at the different ways in which supervisors in the Canadian study treated their male and female subordinates, they were:

- twice as likely to watch and engage in sports with male subordinates;
- three times as likely to engage in non-work-related conversations with male subordinates; and
- more than twice as likely to engage in conversations about current events with male subordianets.

These differences may seem trivial, but together they form a pattern that Herminia Ibarra,[22] in her summary of the networking literature, found to be commonplace and significant. She learned that men are more likely than women with the same education and experience to gain access to the networks of their mentors and to be drawn into key political coalitions. Women, on the other hand, often find themselves straddling two networks: a male-dominated network, which provides greater assistance in their attainment of workplace effectiveness, and a women's network, which provides them with more comfortable social ties. These two groups often subject women to the stress of conflicting advice, forcing them to maintain a delicate balance lest one network reject them because of their commitment to the other. These findings might suggest that, given these conflicts, women would be well advised to seek their social support from other women outside the workplace. In general, however, Ibarra's research summary indicates that same-sex relationships at both the peer and the subordinate-supervisor level provide women with stronger, more satisfying workplace ties than do mixed-sex relationships.

The implication of these few differences is that women and men face very different organisational realities and very different career paths. True, to be part of the group that discusses current events with the boss is a far cry from being promoted, but there is ample evidence to suggest that it is an important step. To be part of the daily discussions is to be privy to titbits of information, and on the accumulation of many such titbits careers have been built.

To see networks from a utilitarian perspective is to see the instrumental value of every interaction. To see networks from a social perspective is to receive another very different kind of gift – that of friendship and support. Women, the literature suggests, tend to be particularly adept at giving and receiving these gifts in the context of networking. Men, seeing networks as utilitarian, are more likely to receive their utilitarian benefits. Women, seeing them as social, may reap mainly social rewards.

There is much to be learned from either approach: the utilitarian value of networking, of gathering information and bestowing favours; and the social value of networking, the joy and the stress-reduction that comes from friendship and support. It is easy for both women and men to see how our own approach is the superior one, a little more difficult to imagine what we could learn by expanding our definitions of networking.

It is worth the effort for managers to encourage and to teach every aspect of networking to their subordinates, to broaden their own vision of the ways in which women and men can work together as task-companions and as friends. Professional associations, in-company networks, women's networks, men's support groups, networks formed of like-minded people of every sex and occupation and level of responsibility – there is room for them all. Men and women are slowly learning to respect their differences and to recognise their similarities. To the extent that they remember this, their networks, whatever they are called, whatever their composition, can aid in the process.

# Notes and References

1. This section draws heavily from Colwill, Nina L. and Vinnicombe, Susan, 'The Case for Women-Only Training: The British and Canadian examples' in Jenny Firth Cozens and Michael West (eds), *Women at Work*, Open University Press, Milton Keynes, 1989, pp. 44–9.

2. Friedman, M. and Rosenman, R. H. *Type A Behavior and Your Heart*, Fawcett Book Group, USA, 1985.
3. Cooper, Cary and Davidson, Marilyn J., *High Pressure; working lives of women managers*, Fontana, 1982.
4. Loden, Marilyn, *Feminine Leadership or How to Succeed in Business Without Being One of the Boys*, Times Books, New York, 1985.
5. Fonda, N., 'Developing Personal Effectiveness: A Course for Women', *Women and Training News*, vol. 15, 1984.
6. Arey, M. L., 'Du Pont Backs Personal Safety with Employee Rape Prevention Program', *Business Health*, 3, 1:56.
7. Vinnicombe, Susan, 'What Exactly Are the Differences in Male and Female Working Styles?', *Women in Management Review*, vol. 3, no. 1, 1987, pp. 13–21.
8. Braiker, H., 'The Type E woman', Naldutton Press, New York, 1987.
9. Schein, Edgar H., *Career Anchors – Discovering Your Real Values*, Pfeiffer & Company, California, USA, 1990.
10. Twelve parts of this section on mentors and protégés borrow from Colwill, Nina L., 'Mentors and protégés, women and men', *Business Quarterly*, Summer 1984, pp. 19–21.
11. Moss Kanter, Rosabeth, *The Change Masters*, London, Routledge, 1991.
12. Kotter, John, *Power and Influence: Beyond formal authority*, The Free Press, 1985.
13. Ritchie, Noreen and Connelly, Michael, 'Mentoring in Public Sector Management: Confronting accountability and control', *Management Education and Development*, vol. 24, no. 2, 1993, pp. 266–79.
14. Colwill, Nina L. and Pollock, Marcy, 'The Mentor Connection Update', *Business Quarterly*, Fall, 1987, pp. 16–20.
15. Spence, J. T., Helmreich, R. L. and Stapp, J., 'The Personal Attributes Questionnaire', *JSAS Catalogue of Selected Documents in Psychology*, vol. 4, 1974, p. 127.
16. Moss Kanter, Rosabeth, *Men and Women of the Corporation*, Basic Books, New York, 1977.
17. Moore, W., *The Conduct of the Corporation*, Random House, New York, 1962.
18. Parts of this section on networking were published as: Colwill, Nina L., 'Understanding the Aspects of Networking', *Women in Management Review*, vol. 5, no. 1, 1995.
19. Paul, Nancy, 'Networking: Women's Key to Success', *Women in Management Review*, Autumn, 1985, pp. 146–51.
20. Zoltie, D. and Clarke, S., 'News and Views', *Women in Management Review*, vol. 8, no. 1, 1993, pp. 31–3.
21. Persaud, Indrani, Sipley, Brenda, Coutts, Brock and Colwill, Nina L., 'Gender Differences in Informal Social Supports: Implications for integrating women into management', Paper presented at the 1990 ASAC Conference, Whistler, BC, June, 1990.
22. Ibarra, Herminia, 'Personal Networks of Women and Minorities in Management: A conceptual framework', *Academy of Management Review*, vol. 8, no. 1, 1993, pp. 56–87.

# 7

# Leadership and Assessment

## Beverly Alimo-Metcalfe

> By valuing a diversity of leadership styles, organizations will find the strength and flexibility to survive in a highly competitive increasingly diverse economic environment.
>
> Judy B. Rosener

Why are there so few women in senior management positions? Why, despite a significant increase in women's employment in management in Europe and the United States over the last 20 years, and notwithstanding equal opportunities and affirmative action legislation, has little or nothing changed? Is it because women are less ambitious, less committed, less educated or less willing to pay the costs that go with senior posts, or is it because those who hold the gate-keeping positions are determined to ward off any possible breeches in the barriers to the top? Whether conscious or not, considered or coincidental, women in management are experiencing more discrimination and, far from the ceiling being constructed of glass, it is increasingly more like reinforced concrete.

## Barriers to equality

Several writers have identified the major barriers to women's representation in senior management as including: the attitudes and behaviour of male managers; search and recruitment methods; selection and assessment methods; and organisational policies and structures that create insurmountable problems for those who care for other family members. This chapter will focus on one of these, namely selection and assessment, which is of particular importance since it reflects both ubiquitous and insidious forms of potential discrimination. Moreover, as organisations are adopting increasingly sophisticated assessment methods, the nature of possible gender bias becomes far more difficult to notice and to challenge.

# Why focus on assessment?

The importance of scrutinising assessment processes is crucial since entry into, and movement up and/or across the organisation, take place as a result of selection and assessment procedures, both formal and informal. In addition, the identification of potential or talent of any employee and the opportunities that they are offered for their development, together with the recognition that they are given for good performance, occur as a result of being assessed, whether by an explicit method, such as an appraisal, or by the more insidious and subtle process of a boss's opinion formation or remarks to others.

This chapter will focus mainly on formal process of assessment but cannot ignore reference to what is known about attitudes to women in management.

# The process of assessment

Assessment of potential and of actual performance in management is clearly a very complex process; however, this is not to assume that it is commonly understood as such in organisations. Whether the organisation is selecting an individual for a management post or identifying individuals with potential for promotion, the three steps of assessment should be clearly understood. In order to explain the potential sources of discrimination for women in management, it is essential to outline the three major stages of the process, since there is possible bias in each of them. Table 7.1 describes these steps.

## Stage one: what are the skills, behaviours and qualities of effective managers?

The first stage is to draw up a list of the knowledge, skills, qualities and experience required for the job. Clearly you need to know exactly what you want to measure, before measuring it. The criteria that emerge at this

**Table 7.1** Stages in the assessment process.

| | |
|---|---|
| Stage 1   Job analysis | Identify criteria required (traits, abilities, qualities) |
| Stage II   Select a predictor/assessment technique | Selection interview psychometric instrument (personality measure, ability test) Appraisal data (including track record) Assessment centre |
| Stage III   Assessors evaluate data | Assessors' judgements |

initial stage form the basis for every subsequent activity, namely the selection of the appropriate assessment technique and making the final decision about the individual.

If we were to focus on the skills and qualities of a senior manager, one source of information might be articles and books on management. The problem here is that almost all research on management and leadership has been conducted on totally male or predominantly male groups of managers. This would not be a matter for concern if there were no evidence that women and men, on average, behave similarly in a managerial role. However, there have been several important research studies over the last few years investigating the nature of leadership which have found that this not to be the case.

Most of these studies have been conducted in the United States and have been undertaken by major academic researchers. Before describing their findings, it is important to recognise the changing shape and nature of modern organisations in a constantly changing world.

In order to survive the turbulent forces of change, the directors of large organisations are realising they must undergo a kind of metamorphosis, transforming themselves from large, multilayered hierarchical structures to slimmer, flatter, decentralised units with people working in multifunctional teams. Managers can no longer rely on status and authority to influence activity but should empower teams to take their own decisions within the framework of the organisation's strategic plan, supported by a learning culture.

The need for constant adaptability means that managers must see that their major responsibility should be the encouragement and support of growth. Managers are, or at least should be, in the development business. If the latest research is to be believed, this is less likely to happen if men dominate senior management.

In a United States study of male and female leaders, Rosener[1] found that men's preferred style of management, described as 'transactional leadership', is concerned with exchanging rewards and punishments for performance. Men were also more likely to use power that comes from their organisational position. Women behaved very differently. They preferred to use a 'transformational' or 'interactive leadership' style that encourages participation, the sharing of power and information and the creation of situations that contribute to people feeling good about themselves. Unlike the men, who wanted to guard their information, women shared it and preferred to seek solutions from staff rather than behaving as though they were 'experts'. Women were also much more likely to admit that they did not have all the answers and to seek criticism, both of which appear, generally speaking, to be unusual behaviours for men.

These findings are particularly important since, in research conducted in a wide variety of organisations, including industry, the military, education, and health care, the use of a transformation style has resulted in staff who show the highest effort, performance and job satisfaction. 'Transformation style' has also been found to relate strongly to organisational morale, team cohesion, commitment, and team and organisational measures of success.[2]

Another American study asked *subordinates* to rate their manager on a leadership style measure.[3] The researchers then analysed the data comparing females and males in terms of the specific transformational and 'transactional leadership' styles. They found that the women displayed more transformational leadership behaviour than did the men.

These findings indicate a potential gender bias in the first stage of assessment, because they imply that one is more likely to come up with descriptions of 'transactional leadership' if one refers to past descriptions of leadership behaviour in textbooks since they were based on studies of men as leaders. Furthermore, given that the commonly adopted method of identifying 'What it is that you are looking for in a manager?', is to ask the opinions of senior managers, 95 per cent of whom are men, it is not surprising that the criteria given describe the male model of transactional leadership.

While the studies cited here have been conducted in the United States, there is evidence that the situation is similar in the United Kingdom. A recent study published of male and female housing managers' gives descriptions of the qualities required for their job.[4] The results demonstrate somewhat similar sex differences. These are shown in Table 7.2.

In a study I am currently conducting with senior female and male managers in the British National Health Service, again, very different descriptions of behaviours and qualities required of effective leaders have been obtained (Table 7.3).[5]

Thus, there appears to be ample support for my concern regarding gender bias in the first stage of assessment and, as we shall see in a later

**Table 7.2** Characteristics sought for in the job of a housing manager by female and male housing managers.

| Aspect | Job 'A': the feminine job | Job 'B': the masculine job |
|---|---|---|
| The priorities they see for the job | • team management central<br>• effective service delivery | • vision<br>• entrepreneurship (i.e. not confined to administering)<br>• ability to package ideas for funding |
| Working style | • people-oriented<br>• works through people<br>• measured<br>• participative | • political<br>• forceful<br>• high profile<br>• flamboyant<br>• confident<br>• aware of external events |
| Decision-making approach | • not snap decisions<br>• familiarises self with key aspects | • paternalistic<br>• quick<br>• action-orientated<br>• detached<br>• analytical<br>• systematic |
| Interpersonal relationships with own team | • understanding of people<br>• sensitivity<br>• care for individual feelings and development<br>• rich perception of human beings | • supports own team<br>• looks after their interests<br>• defends them to the hilt |
| Interpersonal relationships with clients | • empathy<br>• understanding of different needs | • can use pressure groups |

Source: Sparrow and Rigg[4]

section, this may explain, in part, why women are perceived to be less competent in management than are their male counterparts.

## Stage two: the method used to assess management potential

Once the list of managerial criteria has been drawn up, the most appropriate way of measuring these criteria must be decided. With respect to assessment for job selection or for promotion, several techniques may be considered. These include:

• a selection interview;

**Table 7.3** Perceptions of the characteristics of managers with leadership skills in the NHS.

| | Female managers' perceptions | Male managers' perceptions |
|---|---|---|
| Communication and interpersonal skills | • Relates to others on an equal level<br>• Personally approachable (can share personal information and responds at human level)<br>• Fun to be with<br>• Sensitive – has time to notice concerns of others<br>• Conscious of impact of own activities on others<br>• Communicates support of other's point of view<br>• Nurses someone who feels intimidated in meetings | • Confident as a speaker<br>• Able to influence others<br>• At ease with people<br>• Communicates two-way<br>• Can communicate effectively to wide audience |
| Working style | • Creative use of others' skills – for their benefit and organisation's<br>• Busy but accessible<br>• Strong and supportive<br>• Can cope with concept of love in the organisation<br>• Recognises delivery relies on others<br>• Thinks through issues and where they are leading people<br>• Develops teams in which people grow<br>• Concerned to take people with them<br>• Starts with presumption that everyone wants to do a good job | • Drive<br>• Clarity of purpose<br>• Gives clear direction<br>• Independent<br>• Career driven<br>• Organised |
| Additional personal qualities | • Self-aware (comfortable with self)<br>• Good sense of how others see them<br>• Admits vulnerability<br>• Honest with own values<br>• Credibility with people within and outside the organisation | • Ethical values<br>• Relatively few firm views<br>• Open to ideas<br>• Cerebral<br>• Confident |

Source: Alimo[5] Metcalfe.

- psychometric instruments including personality scales and ability tests; and

- assessment centre methodology.

### Selection interview
The selection interview is the most popular assessment choice, and is used in almost all selection events. It is also, generally speaking, the least accurate method. Frequently poorly conducted, it is a minefield of potential prejudice. Assessors tend to make their decision in the first few minutes of an interview and are very resistant to changing their minds, even when information emerges later in the interview to discount early impressions. Furthermore, the interview is highly susceptible to the influence of personal bias and prejudices. An article reviewing several studies relating to sex discrimination identified numerous sources of bias, including the interviewers' perception of 'feminine' dress, physical attractiveness and a female candidate's suitability for a 'masculine' job. Some writers have suggested that bias can be reduced by providing more information on the candidates' skills and experience to the assessor.[6] However, in a more recent study it was found that – while individualising information eliminated sex-typed personality inferences about male and female applicants and affected applicants' perceived job suitability – discrimination was not eliminated. The final outcome was that male applicants were still preferred for the traditionally male job, and female applicants were favoured for the traditional 'female job'.[7]

### Psychometrics: personality scales and ability tests
Since organisations have realised the weakness of the selection interview, they have become increasingly interested in more 'scientific' techniques of assessment, such as psychometrics. The use of psychological tests, currently booming in the United Kingdom, can help to reduce prejudice but only if they are carefully selected and appropriately used. There have been many instances of total misuse or the use of instruments that are hardly more valid than tea leaves. In the hands of inexperienced 'pseudo-experts', they are dangerous because they can destroy an individual's self-esteem, and even career, almost irreversibly. I also have some concerns about their use in relation to potential sex bias. These concerns relate to their design and the way in which scores are interpreted.

Personality instruments are designed on the basis of identifying questions that reflect dimensions that exist in the body of literature relating to personality theory. As stated earlier, most of the research in pre-1980s psychology has derived from studies of men, which are conducted by men, in response to questions proposed by men, and the data analysed from a male perspective.[8] Many, if not most, 'classic' theories of personality were created in this manner. Only relatively recently have writers investigated the existing theories and their methodologies from a perspective of questioning their predominantly male bias.

A good example relates to the concept that is often referred to in organisations: achievement motivation. The research on which the concept is developed was based exclusively on male samples. It is particularly interesting to note that when researchers attempted later to measure achievement motivation in a sample of women, the women responded in ways which were interpreted as their being less motivated than men. However, subsequent research on women found that 'interestingly, the researchers did not seem to think it important that under relaxed conditions females actually scored higher than males . . .' Perhaps more importantly, scholars have looked more closely and critically at the meaning of achievement motivation, and found it to be defined and valued differently by females and males.

A leading Harvard academic, Carol Gilligan, neatly summarised the sometimes subtle nature of sex bias in personality measurement in this cogent manner:

McClelland . . . reports that 'psychologists have found sex differences in their studies from the moment they started doing empirical research' . . . But because it is difficult to say 'different' without saying 'better' or 'worse', and because there has been a tendency to construct a single scale of measurement, and because that scale has been derived and standardised on the basis of men's observations and interpretations of research data predominantly or exclusively drawn from studies of males, psychologists have tended, in McClelland's words, 'to regard male behaviour as the "norm" and female behaviour as some kind of deviation from that norm . . . Thus, when women do not conform to the standards of psychological expectation, the conclusion has been that something is wrong with the women.[9]

Together with other psychologists, I have also expressed concern in relation to the design and scoring (norms) of intelligence tests. As British writer and academic Janette Webb states:

The construction of test items can be manipulated so as to favour one group over another [and that this] has long been known in the sphere of intelligence testing. . . . The IQ debate continues, but there is adequate work to substantiate the argument that the construction of such tests can be manipulated to reproduce, or to undermine, socially approved results for the distribution of intelligence according to class, gender and ethnicity.[10]

It is interesting to remember that in the UK, when girls were found to obtain higher scores on the 11-plus examination for entry to secondary school, the way in which girls and boys were scored was altered in order to ensure similar proportions of passes by sex.

There is also a suggestion that men and women may have different modes of 'rational' thinking. The difference perceived is that men tend to use the approach of linear logic, namely, from A to B to C; whereas women tend to think in a more 'radar' way, that is by scanning many different pieces of information and the way they interconnect. So, for example, a female manager or professional who must work away from home for a few days may think 'I must check whether there is enough food for the children's sandwiches during the week, and Susan needs to be collected by a friend from piano lessons, but as she's afraid of dogs I must remember to ask the friend not to take the dog with her; and since that will be the same day that Peter is staying late at school we need to book a baby-sitter. And as I will not be able to phone on Wednesday as I'll be flying most of the day, which is also David's birthday I need to ask the shop to deliver the present . . .' and so on.

Whether as a resulting evolution, or simply more aware than men of many issues at the same time, it would appear that women may think in more complex, multidimensional ways. None the less, many of the popular intelligence tests being used by organisations as part of the process for selecting managers appear to favour the way in which men tend to think.

Certainly there has been repeated evidence of women scoring more highly on verbal tests of intelligence than do men. However, the converse is generally true for numerical tests. Does verbal ability have a lower status than numerical ability?

**The assessment centre**
The most recent development in assessing managerial potential, the assessment centre, is also the most complex. Despite its name, it does not refer to a specific location or building, but refers to a particular method of assessment. It is based on the logical notion of 'if we want to see if someone can do a job, let's observe them trying to do it'.

With this technique, six or so candidates who may be being considered for a particular job are brought together to undertake group and individual exercises that are designed to simulate important activities of a job. They might serve as members of a team trying to solve a real or hypothetical complex organisational problem; they might be asked to make a presentation to an audience, the members of which can also ask questions; or they might be asked to role-play a manager counselling a member of staff. The candidates are observed in these and other roles by senior managers in the same organisation, who have been trained to assess their behaviours. Clearly, assessment centres can be extremely expensive, both in the cost of the consultants who design the centre and train the managers, and in the cost of individuals' absence from work. Since they are often held in hotels rather than in the workplace, and may last two or three days, they also typically involve high accommodation costs. The reason for their increased popularity in organisations is that they provide the most accurate assessments of individuals' potential, and are used most commonly for senior management selection and to identify high flyers for fast-track career development programmes.

Despite their increased accuracy I have several concerns about possible sources of sex bias in assessment centres. The first relates to the criteria or dimensions that form the basis of the design of the centre. As mentioned above, the observers are usually senior managers in the organisation who are selected and trained in behavioural observation techniques, to rate candidates while observing their performance in a variety of activities. Often, the assessors are given 'behavioural frameworks' or 'guidelines', which contain specific examples of 'above average', 'average' and 'below average' behavioural indicators. If these indicators have emerged from a totally male, or predominantly male group and if there is evidence of gender differences in management style, then clearly these indicators offer potential sources of sex bias.

Deborah Tannen's book[11] on differences in the ways in which women and men communicate highlights the subtleties of sex differences in verbal interaction, which one suspects have yet to be absorbed into the established 'body of knowledge' and general models of interpersonal style and managerial effectiveness. These findings, plus those cited earlier, support the view that the behaviours regarded as 'effective' in assessment centres, the behaviours being used to identify potential for senior management, may be heavily biased towards the masculine way of dealing with situations. The result may be that if women handle situations differently, their behaviours are either ignored or allocated relatively low scores.

Because candidates in assessment centres perform tasks in groups, we should also note possible sources of sex bias in group dynamics. Tasks such as simulating a board of directors working on problem-solving activities are frequently included in assessment centres, as are other examples of group activities. In some instances participants are given a specific role, such as director of finance, and sometimes that of leader. Alternatively, no specific roles are allocated, and leaders are expected to emerge. Evidence exists that women are less likely to emerge as leaders in groups in which there is no specific leader.[12] Among the many factors that might contribute to such an outcome may be those described in the book *Women's Ways of Knowing*.[13] The authors cite research on group dynamics in mixed-sex groups that have debunked the popular mythology that women are excessive talkers and have revealed that women are rendered virtually speechless in mixed-sex conversations;[14] women are silenced by excessive interruptions by men;[15] and women are effectively silenced by their role as 'facilitators' in mixed-sex conversations.[16]

It would not be unreasonable to presume that candidates attending assessment centres for senior management positions were predominantly male. This means that those women who do attend usually find themselves in the minority. Research on the emergence of leaders in groups with different proportions of females and males has found that female and male leaders showed similar and high rates of leadership behaviour when in groups comprised exclusively of members of their own sex. However, female leadership behaviour drops dramatically in male-dominant groups, even in cases where the female was the formal group leader. A study by Finnigan[17] concludes that there are several possible reasons for this phenomenon:

1. The majority sex, namely males, inhibit the contributions of the minority sex, namely females, by restricting their opportunities to contribute. Men tend to ask fewer, and only specific kinds of questions of females; they most frequently ask women for information rather than opinions. As a result, the dominating sex, namely men, may be seen to control the nature of women's input.

2. Women may see themselves as outsiders and therefore hold back from influencing discussion.

3. There are cultural forces that render women's contributions to male-dominant groups as being of low value.

Another study investigating leadership behaviour in mixed-sex groups[18] has the interesting addition of looking at the behaviour of women and men interacting, not in groups, but in pairs, when performing a task together. However, in this study the individuals had also completed a scale that examined their preference to dominate, or to be dominated. The researcher paired females and males who rated themselves high on a dominance scale with females and males who rated themselves low, using combinations of mixed and same-sex dyads. Males who were 'high dominants' adopted the leader role in the majority of cases, regardless of their partner's rating of dominance. However, high dominant women paired with low dominant men assumed the leader role only 20 per cent of the time. This study has been repeated by other researchers who obtained similar findings. However, a more recent study argued that the results were a consequence of the task: when a 'feminine' as opposed to a 'masculine' task was used, the high dominant individual always led, irrespective of their sex. Thus, while dominance is likely to predict leadership roles in same-sex pairs, the nature of the task can influence sex role conflict.[19]

In view of these findings, how would one describe the content of managerial assessment centres with respect to the gender of tasks? Presumably by definition they are mainly male-gendered.

## The judgements of assessors

At this point we need to move away from the sole focus of assessment centres and look at techniques of assessment more broadly. The final stage of any assessment process, which should be quite separate from the data-gathering activity – whether an interview, the observation of an exercise or the interpretation of a score on a psychometric instrument – is making an assessment judgement and decision. This is the stage at which assessors must examine all the information they have gathered and make a final decision as to the candidate's performance and potential. Even at this final stage, and despite evidence of the 'good' performance of a female candidate, bias and prejudice can influence the process. Here we need to look at the research findings of men's views of women. How do men view women's appropriateness for a senior management position? For example, are women equally as ambitious or committed as men?

Research suggests that it depends on whether women or men are asked. In a study conducted in the early 1970s, it was found that men held a stereotyped perception of women as dependent, passive, non-competitive, illogical, less competent and less objective than men. But it also found that men felt it *desirable* for women to be less ambitious.[20]

Another United States study conducted around the same time by Virginia Schein[21] investigated male and female middle managers' perceptions of men and women in general, and whether they related to qualities of effective managers. The results showed that both the men and women saw the qualities of effective managers as closely related to those associated with men. Also, while the women's perceptions of effective managers were significantly associated with female qualities, the men saw no relationship between the qualities of effective managers and those associated with women. Schein concluded from their findings that 'think manager equals think male'.

The significance of these findings is crucial, because when it comes to middle and senior management appointments the assessors, or gate-keepers, are highly likely to be men.

Perhaps attitudes towards women have changed over the last 20 years? Virginia Schein replicated her original study in 1989, wanting to gauge the effect of equal opportunities and affirmative action programmes. Her findings provide depressing reading. The women still perceived the qualities of effective managers and those of women and men to be equally strongly correlated; but *nothing* had changed in men's perceptions of the qualities of effective managers and the qualities of women.[22] Recent cross-cultural studies in Europe have found an identical pattern emerging.[23]

Could it be true that women are less ambitious than men and are motivated differently with respect to work? In 1984 I was involved in a national survey of the career development of British managers. Among the questions we asked were questions about their motivation as a manager.

Our findings were clear: there were few differences among women and men. Moreover, the top five motivators – challenging job, good quality senior managers, opportunity for development, being appreciated and autonomy – were identical. In fact, the women scored significantly *higher* on all five.[24] Despite this fact, it seems that men still believe that women are less interested in these aspects of a job. If this is the case, it will almost inevitably affect their judgements of women's suitability or selection for promotion to senior management posts. How do men, if they hold such views of women as lacking in the qualities required of senior managers, deal with data produced from assessment instruments, or selection interviews, or assessment centres which appear to *contradict* these perceptions?

Psychologists use the term 'cognitive dissonance' to describe what happens when we perceive two apparently conflicting 'truths', as may be the case with competent female managers. Dissonance produces tensions, which we seek to reduce, and one way is to attribute an event to a particular cause. 'Success', then, can be attributed to ability – an 'internal' cause that is a function of the particular person. Alternatively, we can attribute success to 'good luck' or to easy tasks – 'external causes' that are out of the individual's control.

Research has consistently found sex differences in attributions of success and failure: a man's success is usually deemed to be due to his ability, while a woman's success is significantly more likely to be attributed to luck or to effort, to her having worked harder than most people would have had to work to accomplish the same task. Conversely, failure in a man is likely to be attributed to his bad luck and in a woman it is far more likely to be attributed to lack of ability.[25]

This may explain why clear evidence exists that similarly qualified and experienced women receive lower evaluations than men, especially when they are applying for 'out of role' jobs – management, engineering, computing, senior medical appointments and so on. It may also throw light on the disadvantage that women appear to suffer in performance appraisal, which in effect inevitably contains an element of assessment of performance, whether explicit or implicit.

# Sex and appraisal

Few studies that have examined differences in the appraisal experience for women and men have shown consistent evidence bias. A study conducted in the Civil Service in the early 1980s showed that women were far less likely to receive critical feedback from their appraiser than did men.[26] While this may sound like a positive finding, women received lower rates of promotion. It was particularly important, therefore, that women should have received feedback as to why they were not perceived to be as effective as their male colleagues. A study in the United States found similar results.[27]

In a study that I directed of a national sample of 1600 NHS junior managers to top managers, the results were particularly disturbing.[28] Women found the appraisal to be significantly more difficult than did the men with respect to talking freely about what they wanted to discuss, identifying their areas of strength, discussing their relationships with their appraiser, and giving feedback to that person. This pattern of results suggests that the women are considerably disempowered by the appraisal process. These findings are particularly important because judgements made in appraisals can have immediate and far-reaching implications for the individual. They can, for example, involve decisions relating to training and development opportunities and career development; in some organisations they are used as a basis for promotion and pay. The implication for women's career development is therefore potentially considerable.

Furthermore, as organisations are increasingly introducing performance-related pay, there is again considerable concern for women.

## *Performance-related pay for women*

A ruling exists under the EC Equal Pay Directive which states that 'the quality of work carried out by a worker may not be used as a criterion for pay increments where its application shows itself to be systematically unfavourable to women'.

In relation to the contentious issue of performance-related pay (PRP), our study obtained similar findings to those found in other organisations with respect to sex bias in performance ratings. Twice the proportion of men, compared to women, were given the top two ratings, and twice the proportion of women to men occupied the lower bands.[28]

Ours was not the only study to reveal discrimination in PRP. Researchers examining sex bias in universities, the British Civil Service, General Accident and British Telecom have all obtained similar data. The British

Telecom study is particularly revealing since it was also found that among the sample of BT executives there were marked differences in the average PRP awarded to women and men (women received lower awards) *even when the women and men received the same rating of performance*.[29] A further study conducted by the Institute of Manpower Studies of four major organisations in the United Kingdom a manufacturing company, a finance organisation, a catering organisation and a local authority, revealed that:

- women in the finance company felt more dissatisfied than the men with the fairness of performance criteria (particularly if they had a male manager);
- managers value different attributes in men than in women: intelligence, dynamism, energy and assertiveness (for men) versus thoroughness, dependability, organisation and honesty (for women); and
- differences in what was valued for women and men reinforced sex stereotypes.

The authors concluded that 'bias may enter the appraisal and merit pay process at a myriad of points'.[30]

## Gender and career promotion

Finally, if women are not perceived to be as competent as their male colleagues, or as possessing the attributes commonly associated with effective management, this will undoubtedly have profound effects on rates of promotion. Regrettably this, too, is borne out by research.

There have been several studies which have revealed far slower rates of promotion for women than men in the same organisations and specialisms, even when the woman is better qualified. Examples abound in a wide range of professions including management, nursing, education, law, medicine and accountancy.[31] The list is endless.

A recent study in the United States revealed a more disturbing source of discrimination. A group of female and male MBAs were compared with respect to their levels of promotion several years after graduation. Surprisingly, there were no significant differences in the number of promotions but further investigation revealed that the women had attained significantly lower positions of management authority than did the men. It should be noted that variables such as career breaks were controlled for. The women were far more likely to have been promoted within their specialism – a phenomenon called 'pacification by promotion'. Their promotions were hollow since their influence did not increase.[32]

Despite all the disheartening evidence, I am optimistic. We are now at least aware of the potentially 'hidden' discriminators for women.

I will end by returning to one of the most encouraging studies to have emerged in the 1990s, that of Judy Rosener. She conducted her study as a sample of 300 women and 100 men, all of whom were in very senior positions in major US blue chip organisations: Rosener states:

> [Women] are succeeding because of – not in spite of – certain characteristics generally considered to be 'feminine' and inappropriate in leaders.
>
> The women's success shows that a non-traditional leadership style is well suited to the conditions of some work environments and can increase an organisation's chances of surviving in an uncertain world.[33]

The good news is that these women, by adopting transformational leadership styles, are not simply cloning the masculine models of leadership and management that have created such a prevalence of unhealthy organisations, with overstressed, demoralised and disempowered staff, but are bringing with them the real qualities of warmth, consideration for others, nurturance of self-esteem and, above all, integrity.

## Conclusion

In summary, there is growing evidence that the modern style of leadership desperately required for organisations, namely that which embodies vision, individual consideration, strengthening of individuals' involvement in decision-making and nurturance of growth and self-esteem, is more likely to be found in women.

This chapter has argued that as organisations purportedly attempt to increase the fairness and objectivity of assessment process by adopting more sophisticated forms of assessment they may, in fact, be increasing the effect of sex bias. Furthermore, as the techniques of assessment become more complex, sources of bias are far less obvious and hence less likely to be challenged.

## References

1. Rosener, J., 'Ways women lead', *Harvard Business Review*, Nov/Dec, pp. 119–25, 1990.

2. Bass, B. M. and Avolio, B. J., 'Shatter the glass ceiling: women make better managers', *Report 92-1, The Center for Creative Leadership*, p. 19, 1992.
3. Bass, B. M., Avolio, B. J. and Atwater, L., 'The transformational and transactional leadership of men and women: an extension of some old comparisons', *Report 93–6, The Center for Leadership Studies*, School of Management, State University of New York at Binghampton, 1993.
4. Sparrow, J. and Rigg, C., 'Job analysis: selecting for the masculine approach to management', *Selection and Development Review*, vol. 9, no. 2, pp. 5–8, 1993.
5. Alimo-Metcalfe, B., 'An investigation of female and male constructs of leadership and empowerment', Paper presented at the 23rd International Congress of Applied Psychology, Madrid, 17–22 July 1994.
6. Nieva, V. F. and Gutek, B., 'Sex effects of evaluation', *Academy of Management Review*, vol. 5, no. 2, pp. 267–76, 1980.
7. Glick, P., Zion, C. and Nelson, C., 'What mediates sex discrimination in hiring decisions?', *Journal of Personality and Social Psychology*, vol. 55, no. 2, pp. 178–86, 1988.
8. Jacobson, S. W. and Jacques, R., 'Of knowers, knowing and the known: a gender framework for revisioning organizational and management scholarship', Paper presented at the Academy of Management Annual Meeting, San Francisco, 10–12 August 1990.
9. Gilligan, C., *In A Different Voice: Psychological Theory and Women's Development*, Harvard University Press, Boston, 1982.
10. Webb, J., 'Gendering selection psychology', *The Occupational Psychology*, vol. 3, December 1987, pp. 4–5.
11. Tannen, D., *You Just Don't Understand: Women and Men in Conversation*, Virago, London, 1992.
12. Megargee, E. I., 'Influence of sex roles in the manifestation of leadership', *Journal of Applied Psychology*, vol. 53, pp. 317–82, 1969.
13. Belenky, M. F., Clinchy, B. M. and Goldberger, N. R., *Women's Ways of Knowing: The Development of Self, Voice and Mind*, Basic Books, New York, 1986.
14. West, C. and Zimmerman, D. H., 'Small insults: a study of interruptions in cross-sex conversations between unacquainted persons', In Thorne, B., Kramarea, C. and Henley, N. (eds), *Language, Gender and Society*, Newbury House, Rowley, MA, 1993, pp. 103–18.
15. Zimmerman, D. H. and West, C., 'Sex roles, interruptions, and silences in conversation' in Thorne, B. and Henley, N. (eds), *Language and Sex: Difference and Dominance*, Newbury House, Rowley, MA, 1975, pp. 105–30.
16. Fishman, P., 'Interaction: the work women do' in Thorne, B., Kramarea, C. and Henley, N. (eds), *Language, Gender and Society*, Newbury House, Rowley, MA, 1983, pp. 89–102.
17. Finnigan, N., 'The effects of token representation on participants in small decision-making groups', *Economic and Industrial Democracy*, vol. 3, 1983, pp. 531–50.
18. Megargee, E. I., 'Influence of sex roles in the manifestation of leadership', *Journal of Applied Psychology*, vol. 53, 1969, pp. 317–82.

19. Carbonell, J. L., 'Sex roles in the manifestation of leadership', *Journal of Applied Psychology*, vol. 69, 1984, pp. 44–9.
20. Broverman, I. K., Vogel, R., Broverman, D. M., Clarkson, F. E. and Rosenkrantz, P. S., 'Sex roles stereotypes: a current appraisal' in Schuch Mednick, M. T., Tangri, S. S. and Hoffman, L. W. (eds), *Women and Achievement: Social and Motivational Analyses*, Hemisphere Publishing, New York, 1975.
21. Schein, V., 'Relationships between sex role stereotypes and requisite management characteristics among female managers', *Journal of Applied Psychology*, vol. 60, 1975, pp. 340–44.
22. Schein, V. and Mueller, R., 'Sex role stereotyping and requisite management characteristics: a cross cultural look', Paper presented at the 22nd International Congress of Applied Psychology, 22–27 July 1989, Kyoto.
23. Orser, B., 'Sex role stereotypes and requisite management characteristics: an international perspective', *Women in Management Review*, vol. 9, no. 4, 1994, pp. 11–19.
24. Alban-Metcalfe, B. M., 'What motivates managers? An investigation by gender and sector of employment', *Public Administration*, vol. 678, no. 1, 1989, pp. 95–108.
25. Wallston, B. S. and O'Leary, V. E., 'Sex makes a difference: differential perceptions of women and men', In Whitter, L. (ed.), *Reviewing Personality and Social Psychology*, vol. 2, 1981, pp. 9–41.
26. Corby, S., *Equal Opportunities for Women in the Civil Service*, HMSO, London, 1982.
27. Thomas, P. J., 'Appraising the performance of women: gender and the naval officer' in Gutek, B. A. and Larwood, L. (eds), *Women's Career Development*, Sage, London, 1982.
28. Alimo-Metcalfe, B., 'Gender and appraisal: findings from a national survey of managers in the British health service', Paper presented at the Global Research Conference on Women in Management, 21–23 October 1992, Ottawa, Canada.
29. Society of Telecom Executive *Stressing Performance*, STE Research, London, 1992.
30. Bevan, S. and Thompson, M., *Merit Pay, Performance Appraisal and Attitudes to Women's Work*, Institute of Manpower Studies, Sussex, 1992.
31. Davidson, M. J. and Burke, R. (eds), *Women in Management: Current Research Issues*, Paul Chapman Publishing, London, 1994.
32. Flanders, D. P. and Anderson, P. E., 'Sex discrimination in employment: theory and practice', *Industrial and Labour Relations Review*, vol. 26, 1973, pp. 938–55.
33. Rosener, J., 'Ways women lead', *Harvard Business Review*, Nov.–Dec., 1990, pp. 119–25.

# 8

# Strategies for Change – Company Cases

## Susan Vinnicombe and Jane Sturges

> Of course the glass ceiling is still in existence in some companies.
> In others there's a bit of melting going on.
>
> Lady Howe, Chairman of Opportunity 2000

There is no current *Which?* guide evaluating companies' policies on women in management yet; but an 18-month research survey conducted by Scarlett McGuire in the United Kingdom in 1992 highlights the best companies for women. The research shows that companies are now more keen to retain women after they leave to have children. 'Mothers in those companies spoke of the difference between formerly being allowed back to do part-time work and now being allowed to follow a career again.'[1]

A surprising finding of the survey is that some of Britain's biggest engineering and chemical companies emerge from the study well. Only one union, NALGO, made it into the list which is dominated by retail chains, the media, finance companies and local authorities.

The top 15 companies for women according to the study[1] are as follows:

Civil Service
Marks & Spencer
Ove Arup
Sainsbury
Littlewoods
Shell
LWT

110

BP
Esso
Mars
British Rail
NatWest
Legal and General
BBC
Channel 4

The Civil Service comes out top for its broad range of services including career breaks, job-shares, crèches and flexible hours. Rank Xerox, Barclays Bank, BT and the Co-op Bank are four companies which have set about establishing equal opportunity programmes in different ways and form case studies for companies looking for strategies for fostering women in management.

## Rank Xerox – removing stereotypes

Formed in 1956 as a joint venture between Xerox Corporation and the Rank Organisation, Rank Xerox manufactures and markets document processing products and services throughout Europe, Asia and Africa.

Its UK subsidiary, Rank Xerox (UK) Ltd was set up in 1972 and now employs a total of 4500 people in 50 locations throughout the United Kingdom. It markets Xerox products and services in the United Kingdom and Ireland through a direct sales force and an indirect sales network through Rank Xerox Business Services, which manages Xerox Copy Centres, and through Xerox Office Supplies.

Thirty per cent of Rank Xerox (UK)'s employees are women. This percentage has grown from 25 per cent in 1989, when the company introduced its equal opportunities initiative under the banner of its corporate equality statement 'We only discriminate on ability'.

The main purpose of the initiative, however, has not been simply to bring more women into Rank Xerox, but to balance their representation in certain areas, in particular in sales and management. (As in most other companies, in the past men within Rank Xerox performed certain jobs and women others, with very little cross-over between the two.) To this end it had been very successful: the number of women sales executives has grown from 15 per cent in 1989 to 28 per cent in 1994, and the number of women managers has increased in the same period from 10 per cent to 17 per cent.

Rank Xerox believes that employing more women in sales roles will not only improve the ratio of the sexes in this area but will also increase the number of women managers it employs in the longer term: internal analysis has shown that sales roles are the traditional source for Rank Xerox managers, with many having significant experience of sales and marketing. To this end, management want to see the percentage of women it recruits to sales jobs rise more than 40 per cent.

Improving the number of women in sales jobs has been one part of an initiative at Rank Xerox to remove the stereotypes which in the past have surrounded certain jobs within the organisation. Sales was traditionally seen as a 'male' area, as was customer engineering, where women account for only 0.5 per cent of staff. On the other hand, when Rank Xerox undertook its equality initiative in 1989, the vast majority of professional and support staff were women.

Management felt that for equal opportunities to be addressed in a meaningful way, the 'glass walls' categorising certain jobs as 'male' or 'female' would have to be removed. It has attempted to do this in a hard-hitting 'positive action' recruitment advertising campaign which it has run in the national and local press for the past five years, when seeking to recruit in three particular areas.

The campaign consists of three separate advertisements, which attempt to recruit women to customer engineer and sales executive posts and men to support staff positions by openly questioning the legitimacy of the stereotypes which surround these jobs. All the advertisements feature Rank Xerox's corporate equality statement 'We only discriminate on ability' as a copy line.

The advertising campaign has succeeded in persuading more people of the opposite sex to apply for jobs traditionally stereotyped as being male or female, especially male-biased sales jobs. (The numbers of women taking up jobs as customer engineers has not increased to the same extent as the increase in sales jobs because there has been little recruitment in this area since the advertising was launched.) Rank Xerox continues to run what it describes as its 'positive action' recruitment advertising whenever the need arises.

Rank Xerox sees its equal opportunities programme as an initiative that will help it to maximise its competitive potential, not something which it is doing simply because it feels it ought to. Furthermore, by relating equal opportunities to its current and future business needs the company has made it a central concern of all its managers and employees, and not only its human resources department. At its inception, more than 60 one-day equality workshops were held for Rank Xerox's 500 most senior managers, who themselves generated a number of commercial reasons why it was important for the organisations to endorse equal opportunities. These included the need to recruit and keep the best staff and the need to improve customer relations. The equality workshop concept was then cascaded down through the whole of Rank Xerox over the next two years, so that all staff understood and supported the need for equal opportunities.

The attempt to create equal opportunity by removing stereotypes at Rank Xerox has been reinforced by other initiatives aimed at helping women to obtain and to retain management positions. The company has revised its succession planning process so that all women above first-level management are automatically considered. It has introduced the concept of flexible working for women and men at all levels, including management, within the organisation.

Surveys among Rank Xerox female employees have indicated that they would prefer the opportunity to work flexibly after having had a child, rather than be given an extended period of maternity leave. Management is now prepared to allow employees to work as flexibly as they wish, as long as the flexibility they choose meets Rank Xerox's business needs as well. The results of this policy have been astonishing. Between 80 per cent and 90 per cent of women now return to work after the birth of a child, compared with a previous figure of only 20 per cent. The criterion for career breaks has been reduced from five years to two.

To support its equal opportunity initiatives the company has developed and implemented a measurement system for assessing its progress, based on a seven-step assessment process; this has been fully integrated into the annual inspection of business performance.

Unlike many British organisations, Rank Xerox has unashamedly set goals for the number of women managers. Management want women to occupy 25 per cent of managerial jobs by the end of 1995.

Achieving this target will not be easy. The UK company has undergone a significant organisational change programme as part of Rank Xerox's worldwide strategy. The change programme has involved a delayering exercise, removing a large number of managerial positions overall and thereby reducing the scope of the company to encourage more women into management.

Nevertheless, the Rank Xerox equal opportunities programme will continue at the same pace as before. The company has begun an initiative seeking feedback from employees at all levels and plans next to undertake a new programme of diversity workshops for leaders and decision-makers. These will conclude with a board level planning workshop, with the aim of building the Rank Xerox diversity strategy for the year 2000.

# Barclays Bank – flexible work for the caring majority

Barclays Bank is one of the 'Big Four' clearing banks in the United Kingdom, offering a complete range of consumer and business banking services through its network of 2000 branches. Like the other major banks, commercial and technological pressures have forced it to reduce its staff considerably over the past five years; nevertheless, it still employs a total of 65 000 people in the United Kingdom.

Traditionally Barclays has employed large numbers of women: 65 per cent of its current staff are female. However, the nature of past job segregation in the banking industry has meant that until recently most were employed in clerical positions, while as many as 95 per cent of staff at managerial level were men.

Thanks to a number of measures introduced during the past few years, 15 per cent of Barclays' managers are now women. (It should be noted that many branch managers are in fact graded as senior clerical staff in the bank. If their numbers were included in Barclays' statistics on women managers, the overall figure would be far higher.)

Central to Barclays' attempts to increase the number of women managers in its organisation has been its attitude to flexible working. The company's past adherence to standard patterns on full-time 35-hour week working for all but the most junior staff is now being broken down at all levels of the organisation. There have been two interlinked reasons for this: first, that Barclays realises the importance of offering flexible working arrangements if it is to retain and promote women, since women's careers still tend to be complicated by the additional burden of family responsibilities; and secondly, an acknowledgement that flexible working practices can help it become more competitive in an environment where financial institutions are increasingly expected to offer a service outside the hours of the traditional working day. It was this argument based on competition which convinced the bank's senior executives that its traditional approach to working arrangements no longer suits the needs of the business, as well as the needs of the staff, and has provided a commercial rationale for Barclays becoming a 'family-friendly' organisation.

Barclays management believes that training and development courses are an important means of getting women into junior management grades but that for women managers to want to stay with the organisation in the long term, flexible working arrangements must be made available. The decision to emphasise this form of help for women within the bank was made after Barclays took part in the National Careers Survey in 1990 and carried out its own research into the subject at the same time.

Barclays found that 65 per cent of its staff had caring responsibilities for children and 38 per cent for elderly relations; some had dual responsibilities. Both male and female employees said that what they sought more than anything else was flexible working arrangements.

The findings were presented to a group of senior line managers at a workshop, which was then used to generate ideas about measures that could be introduced to help Barclays staff combine their careers with their roles as carers. Following on from this, a raft of flexible working measures have been introduced over the past four years.

The company now offers an extra three months unpaid parental leave for new parents, after statutory maternity leave has been taken. The right to this unpaid leave was extended to fathers in 1994.

A job-share scheme has been introduced in an attempt to make part-time working acceptable within higher levels of the organisation. (Junior staff have always been able to work part time if they wished, but it has not, until recently, been an option for employees at managerial grades.) This is seen as the key to breaking down the convention that 'proper' managers always work a 35-hour-plus week. While the scheme is still in its infancy, some senior jobs are already being done on a part-time basis and there are examples of job-sharers being jointly considered for promotion.

Barclays introduced emergency carers leave in 1991. Staff may take up to five days' unpaid leave to look after a dependent child or adult.

A holiday float scheme allows five days' holiday entitlement to be carried forward each year, which can then be used as extra holiday or as an alternative to emergency carers leave.

A responsibility break scheme has been introduced to allow staff with responsibility for elderly, sick or disabled people to take a complete break from work or to work on a temporary part-time basis if necessary. This can last for up to six months and the jobs of those who take advantage of the scheme are guaranteed.

Barclays management believes that the measures it has introduced so far have not only seen the current number of women managers rise but are likely to have an even greater impact in the future: it estimates that 50 per cent of staff at the grade immediately below management are women and it is from this grade that managers are drawn. As a result, 39 per cent of staff gaining their first managerial appointment are now women.

At the same time, since the company has introduced its flexible working arrangements the number of women returning from maternity leave has doubled. Whereas two-thirds of Barclays' female employees used to leave the organisation when they had a child, now two-thirds remain, many of whom choose to work part time. The bank anticipates that the number of women taking advantage of its flexible working schemes is likely to increase sharply in the near future. The average age of a woman taking maternity leave in Barclays is 29 years and the age profile of its staff is currently skewed, so that a large number of female staff are aged between 25 and 30.

The company's efforts to retain and promote more women managers are reinforced by a women-only training programme, in operation since 1988. Known as career skills development training and developed with the help of an outside consultant, this has proved to be the most popular course run by Barclays' training department; it has also resulted in some very positive feedback from the women who have attended it, many of whom have said that it has acted as a catalyst in enabling them to take charge of their careers within the bank.

The women's career skills development course was run initially for women in junior management grades but its success meant that it is now also available to women in senior clerical grades, in order to help them move up into managerial jobs; it has also been used for women recruited on to the bank's fast-track programme.

Barclays has supported its equal opportunities initiatives with the introduction of an objective selection method, which takes no account of sex, marital status, age or ethnic origin. In addition its equal opportunities policies are continuously monitored by a computer-based system which checks that they are being implemented correctly.

## BT – developing women managers

For the past eight years the global telecommunications company British Telecom (BT) has run a highly successful series of development programmes designed to promote the careers of its women managers.

BT management's motives for developing its women managers include a desire to build a more balanced workforce which reflects its markets and customer base and a wish to strengthen its management team through a partnership between men and women. They also want to recognise the needs of every employee, in order to involve fully all BT people in the achievement of its business objectives.

At the core of BT's efforts to develop its female employees is a management development course created specifically for women: the company believes that such a programme is the best way of assisting women's career progress within BT. There were three main reasons for choosing this strategy: enlightened business practice was forcing it to look more closely at women's careers in BT; management development was seen as something which had its own intrinsic value; and it was perceived that such a development programme would help BT make better use of its resources.

Despite the spectacular reduction in the BT workforce by 40 000 employees during the early 1990s, BT has maintained and enhanced its women's development programme. Specialised 'training' for women was seen as a key factor in working towards equality for men and women in management. As a result, the format and content of its programme was based on an analysis of what women themselves said they needed, combined with BT's own business needs. Subjects covered include personal development, career planning, assertiveness, developing political skills, leadership and balancing a career with home life.

It was important that the programme be run by women tutors specifically for women, because many women lacked confidence in their own ability and potential, and would feel safer and more comfortable discussing issues around the subject of being a woman manager in an all-female environment.

The heart of the development programme has been a course aimed at women in middle management positions within BT, run for the company by Cranfield School of Management. The first course took place in 1986 and it has run ever since; an estimated total of 600 women have now been through the programme and it continues to be one of BT's most oversubscribed training courses, with demand sometimes three times as high as the number of places available. (The course takes place three times a year.)

The programme is similar to many others which have been run for both male and female managers in terms of the key issues addressed. Where it differs dramatically, however, is in the philosophy which underpins it. Cranfield's work with BT's women managers is based on a belief in the depth and positive potential of the participants and a desire to release such untapped potential as exists within them. This belief is strengthened on the programme by using a bioenergetic framework as a means of increasing self-awareness and understanding.

Bioenergetics is derived from the Reichian school of philosophy: as a psychological model it attempts to help people to come to terms with and understand themselves by considering how their personalities manifest themselves in both their minds and their bodies.

The bioenergetic model is used on the BT programme not to show the women managers who they are, but to help identify blocks which stop them from being who they can be, and pull out their potential beyond their own definition of their personality: the Cranfield programme is predicated on an acceptance that people can expand beyond their apparent limitations, which are often nothing more than the result of mechanisms to cope with the external environment.

As well as the course for women in middle management, BT now also runs two other programmes to develop its women managers: an in-house course for first-line managers, aimed at enabling individuals to identify their strengths and the personal barriers which prevent them from maximising their potential; and a programme for senior managers, also run by Cranfield tutors, and intended to develop strategic skills.

Research by Cranfield itself and feedback within BT have both shown reactions to the BT women's development programme to be very positive. Cranfield carried out its own evaluation in 1989, sending questionnaires to participants, their partners, their line managers and their subordinates. The research, which elicited a very high response rate, found that the programme's three areas of greatest impact on participants, according to the participants themselves, their partners and their line managers, were personal development, career planning and managerial effectiveness. These findings reflect BT's objectives in setting up the programme, which were to develop such characteristics in its women managers.

Feedback about the course within BT itself is also very positive. BT carries out extensive research to determine how the programme has affected course participants, what things they have done differently as a result of attending a course and what part of it made the most impact on them. A survey among those who had participated in the programmes during 1992 and 1993 found that the positive outcomes of attending the courses included better self-awareness, improved relationships with others, increased confidence, a better understanding of career planning and greater assertiveness.

The results of attending BT's women development programme are increased self-awareness, which then leads to higher levels of confidence and assertiveness, and finally results in an improved ability in handling relationships with others. This, BT believes, increases its women managers' personal effectiveness and makes them able to make a greater contribution to the business.

One important spin-off of the women's development programme at BT has been the establishment of a BT Women's Network. This was set up in 1987 by those who participated in the very first Cranfield course. The network is now an important independent voice within BT, with its own committee, newsletter and programme of meetings with visiting speakers.

BT's commitment to its development programme for women managers has been backed up since the late 1980s by other measures aimed at helping all its employees, male and female, to balance their work and home commitments. These include flexible working and job-sharing initiatives, as well at BT's first workplace nursery.

As well as maintaining its support for the existing women-only programme, BT's latest initative is to introduce a new programme for men and women, which will deal with issues related to men and women in the workplace such as working together more effectively, building better working relationships and valuing individual diversity.

# Co-operative Bank – levelling the playing field

The Co-operative Bank is a medium-sized UK retail bank, based in Manchester and employing approximately 3500 people nationwide. It operates exclusively within the UK banking market where it offers a full range of banking services, including telephone banking, to both personal and business customers. While it cannot compete with the United Kingdom's 'Big Four' banks on size alone, it does enjoy certain market niches: for example, it has a 30 per cent share of the local authority banking market.

Nevertheless, like all UK banks, it has experienced dramatic changes in recent years as the effects of the recession have accelerated the wide-ranging technological changes which were already taking place in the banking industry. Competition has increased from foreign banks, building societies and retailers and customer requirements have changed: the Co-operative Bank has been forced to adopt a much sharper commercial focus as a result.

The key challenge the bank has faced has been to retain and develop its customer base and the strategy it has chosen to adopt has been to do this by providing top quality and accessible service to its customers at an acceptable cost to itself.

Central to this strategy is its human resources policy. The high levels of service that management wants to offer its customers requires that it retains and develops its best staff to their fullest potential, regardless of whether they are male or female. The role that they play in the delivery of services the bank offers is recognised as crucial to its success.

In the past the Co-operative Bank, like other banks, has tended to under-use the resources of its female employees. While female equality is explicitly stated in its mission statement, until recently few of its managers were women. Women comprised around 60 per cent of the bank workforce, yet most of these staff were concentrated on clerical positions, where women occupied about 80 per cent of jobs. At the supervisory level women more or less had parity with men, but they were heavily outnumbered in managerial and senior managerial grades.

In the new more competitive commercial environment the Co-operative Bank began to realise that it could no longer afford to overlook the potential of its female staff, for commercial as well as ethical reasons. If it was to offer the best service possible it needed to employ the best staff, based on their abilities, not their sex. Furthermore, half its customers were female, and therefore a situation in which most managers did not reflect the bank's client base existed.

Getting women into management was seen as a particular challenge and the approach that the bank took was one which aimed to 'level the playing field' and remove any advantages which male employees may have enjoyed by virtue of their sex in the past. At the heart of this initiative was the Co-operative Bank's adoption of a 'genderless' approach to employee recruitment and retention.

Central to the 'genderless' approach is a promotions policy based on whether candidates possess particular competencies the bank has defined that it requires for management positions, not on other, more subjective criteria. The competency approach was first taken when, in 1992, a restructure of the Co-operative Bank's branch network meant that the bank had to re-select staff for all its branches, including branch manager jobs. A model was developed for the new type of bank manager the Co-operative Bank was looking for, which comprised seven distinguishing competencies. These were:

Initiative

Thoroughness

Good planning

Results focused

Empathy

Teamworking

Good product knowledge

The re-selection method used was an assessment centre designed to test for these competencies. The outcome of the exercise was that the Co-operative Bank ended up with 20 per cent more women branch managers than previously and the position of the new female managers was strengthened by the fact that they had been chosen purely on merit.

The bank has now identified the key management competencies which it believes operate in all its managerial jobs and published them, with appropriate weightings, in the form of job profiles. These form the basis of its key human resource practices, including selection, training and development, promotions, and pay and reward. Management believes that the skills which it has identified in the form of competencies reflect a shift in emphasis for managers from an adversarial to a more collaborative style of management, a shift which may also encourage more women to move into management.

The competency-based approach to promotion is backed by other initiatives aimed at improving women's positions in the Co-operative Bank. The organisation has introduced a performance-related pay scheme. In a pilot scheme for telesales staff, women made more calls and sold more products than their male colleagues in an average week, for which they earned more money. The scheme also showed that there was no difference in the number of days lost through sickness, despite the fact that 80 per cent of the women and none of the men had a caring responsibility for young children.

The Co-operative Bank management sees that truly objective pay and reward systems of this kind, based on appropriate performance measures, will benefit women, including women managers, whose average pay still tends to be below that of their male colleagues. An important part of the philosophy underpinning the move towards objective pay systems is that recognising individual women's true value at work in this way should make them more confident about asking for, and being granted, flexible working patterns and career breaks, which to date have not proved particularly popular with women managers.

The bank has a genderless approach to family-friendly working policies, which include flexible working, offering job-sharing and flexible hours, as well as a career break scheme. This scheme allows employees to take short-term breaks, including paternity leave, of up to three months, and long-term breaks for up to five years. Most people who have taken advantage of the long-term scheme so far have used it for child-care purposes.

Among other objectives which the bank has, it hopes that by encouraging more women managers to take advantage of such schemes it will be able to retain and develop their valuable skills, and through this improve the service which it offers its customers.

# References

1. McGuire, Scarlett, *Best Companies for Women*, Pandora Press, London, 1992.

# 9

# Strategies for Change: Women in Management in the United Arab Emirates

## John Bank and Susan Vinnicombe

> There always comes a moment in time when a door opens and lets the future in.
>
> Graham Greene

When oil production first began in Abu Dhabi in 1962, the country lacked schools, hospitals, ports, airports, proper housing, electricity plants and had not a single mile of tarmac road. Thirty-two years later, the United Arab Emirates (UAE) is a modern and developed society with both the infrastructure and the social organisations required to meet the needs of its citizens. Substantial oil revenues have made such a splendid and rapid transformation possible. (The United Arab Emirates controls 4 per cent of the world's oil reserves.) The vision and leadership for such a change was provided by one person – President Sheikh Zayed Bin Sultan Al Nahayan, ruler of the largest emirate, Abu Dhabi, since 1966 and President of the United Arab Emirates since its formation in 1971. He has overseen the transformation of the United Arab Emirates from a single economy, based upon rudimentary agriculture, fishing, pearl-diving and coastal trade, to a complex nation state assuming a leadership role in the Gulf.

Not only have the economics of the United Arab Emirates been irreversibly altered in the last three decades, but social attitudes have also undergone change. One of these remarkable social changes has been a movement towards the emancipation of women.

This case study will discuss the representation of women in UAE management, the reasons why women are taking up careers in management, the barriers hindering women's progress and the actions need to be taken to help UAE women achieve greater gains.

We will begin our examination of the role of women in management in the United Arab Emirates by using the 'force field analysis', an analytical tool that lays bare the dynamics of change. Based on a principle of physics that an object remains static when driving forces and resisting forces are in equilibrium, the technique suggests that in order to change the status quo, driving forces must be strengthened and increased and resisting forces, wherever possible, eliminated or diminished.

# The driving forces for change

There are eight major driving forces acting for change: nationalisation, primacy of education, national wealth, women's associations, favourable work day design, a family-friendly national culture, support for child-care arrangements and changing women's attitudes. Each of these driving forces will be examined for its impact and the ways in which that impact can be increased (see Figure 9.1).

## Nationalisation

The government is committed to a programme of nationalisation, of which the declared purpose is to replace expatriates with UAE nationals wherever possible. At present, with a labour force of more than 794 000 in 1993 and a population of only 2.1 million, the United Arab Emirates is highly dependent on all its adult workers. The President has invested significantly in the development of its human resources in the hopes of creating a skilled indigenous workforce. Compared to expatriates, locals receive preferential treatment in their selection, training, career development and retirement packages. Unlike in the West, where constant down-sizing of organisations and long recessions have hampered women's progress into management, the United Arab Emirates offers good and reliable opportunities for women.

One of the tools used to speed nationalisation in the Abu Dhabi Company for Onshore Oil Operations (ADCO), the onshore arm for oil production of the United Arab Emirates, is 'fast-track' management education. ADCO, like any other Gulf Cooperation Council (GCC) oil company, has had a long history of preparing national employees to assume job responsibilities within the oil industry. The educational activities used in the fast-track programme range through basic vocational and trade training to executive management programmes. Selection to the current programme is based on consistently good annual appraisal ratings.

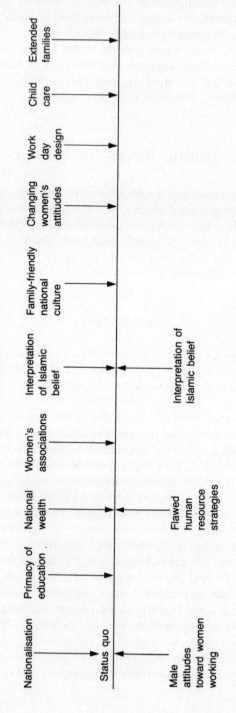

**Figure 9.1** Women in management in Abu Dhabi and the United Arab Emirates: force field analysis.

Twenty-six individuals from professional staff grades are on the programme, administered by the Development and Training Department. Their ages range from late twenties to early forties.

All participants receive personal development plans especially prepared for them. During the process of preparing these plans two major points are specified:

1. No promises of promotion are given (yet within a year all employees selected for the programme had earned one level of promotion, and several had advanced two levels).

2. Inclusion is not lifelong, but depends on the incumbents' continuing to show potential for advancement.

This selection criteria worked so well that it was used for a further group of high-potential nationals. The programme included team building, a leadership module in the outdoors and negotiating skills. Although it is exactly this kind of programme that young women managers in the United Arab Emirates need to help them to assert themselves in the organisation, no local women managers have yet been nominated for this fast-track programme. There are cultural problems in the Arab countries of women mixing with men on residential training programmes, but these problems could be alleviated through the use of women-only programmes.

## Primacy of education

H. H. Sheikh Zayed Bin Sultan Al Nahayan has said that, 'Money is of no use unless it is put to the service of the people'. He goes further, stressing that oil revenues are not ends in themselves, but merely tools. 'The youth are the real wealth of the county', he said. In keeping with this statement, education is the highest priority of the UAE government and absorbs the largest part of its non-defence expenditure, well over 15 per cent of the federal budget. When the United Arab Emirates was established in 1971, the country had only 60 schools with less than 28 000 students. There are now more than 500 government schools with nearly 300 000 students. By the year 2000 illiteracy, which was estimated at 16.8 per cent in 1992–3, should be negligible.

Further education, again free, is provided for the country's citizens in the Emirates university at Al Ain, which was founded in 1977. In 1992 almost 12 000 students graduated for an annual growth rate of 21.2 per cent. There are also more than 1800 students in a growing network of Higher Colleges of Technology across the United Arab Emirates.

Government expenditure on education rose from Dh. 81.5 million in 1972–3 to Dh. 3439 million in 1992–3, an annual growth rate of 20.6 per cent.

In social terms, one of the major changes that has taken place in the Emirates has been the opening of educational opportunities for women. The President, His Highness Sheikh Zayed, has put on record his own view of the subject of equal opportunities. He insists that 'Women have the right to work everywhere' and he insists that this might be exercised without losing traditional respect for women.

The choice to pursue educational courses has been made by thousands of women who are keen to pursue professional careers. Since 1986 female graduates have outnumbered male graduates two to one at the Emirates university. Up to the academic year 1992–3, the university had produced nearly 7000 female graduates. Speaking at the tenth annual Women's Convocation at Al Ain University Her Highness Sheikha Fatma, wife of the President, said, 'The tree of education and advancement planted by His Highness the President is bearing fruit, especially for women.'

## National wealth

Few countries have experienced development at such a pace as has the United Arab Emirates during the past two decades. There have been great economic achievements and far-reaching changes in the way people live. Virtually every aspect of life has changed. The people enjoy a standard of living that is among the highest in the world. During the two decades from 1977 to 1991, the country's gross domestic product (GDP) rose by 16.7 per cent per year, one of the highest growth rates in the world. In 1971 the GDP was Dh. 6.9 billion; in 1992 it rose to Dh. 130.1 billion.[1] The bulk of the United Arab Emirates' income is from oil and 64 per cent of that oil income derives from Abu Dhabi, the richest of the seven Emirates.[2]

The UAE workforce has grown by 8.7 per cent per annum over the past 20 years. Women are beginning to take up professions in the United Arab Emirates but, because money *per se* is less important to them personally than it is to women in the United Kingdom, they can take more time in selecting the 'ideal' job. The majority of students graduating from the Abu Dhabi's Women's Higher College of Technology take two years to find a job at the end of their studies. They favour jobs in the public sector or in the administration of national oil companies, where the traditional hours of employment – 7.00 a.m. to 2.00 p.m. – fit well with their family obligations.

## Women's associations

The Women's Federation was started in the United Arab Emirates in 1975, chaired by H.H. Sheikha Fatma Bint Mubarak. There are eight branches in Abu Dahbi and one branch in five other key towns.

### Objects of the association

The Women's Federation has five primary objectives:

1. To promote the Arab woman spiritually, educationally and socially to enable her to participate in developing her country guided by Islamic teachings.
2. To extend the activity of the association to cover all the Emirates of the State.
3. To support the national rebirth which prevails in the country and to participate in its success by shouldering the responsibilities and performing the duties suitable to her nature in her capacity as a sister, wife and efficient member of the society.
4. To establish close relationships with the women's associations and societies in the Gulf and Arab countries.
5. To follow up activities of Women's Associations in the state and cooperate with them in respect of matters which conform with the nature and objects of the association.

### Methods for achieving objectives

In order to achieve these objectives the following methods were specified:

1. To encourage the establishment of women's societies throughout the United Arab Emirates, to join and cooperate with the association.
2. To cooperate with the members' Women's societies in order to coordinate their activites and evaluate their capacities, so as to provide them with any experience or assistance to achieve their objects and those of the association.
3. To form women's committees at the association level and to maintain full-time experts to help the member societies in carrying on a variety of activities, religious, cultural, health, technical, sports or educational.
4. To cooperate with various government authorities, particularly with Ministry of Education, Social Affairs, Justice and Islamic Affairs and Information.

5. To maintain continuous liaison with Arab women's establishments and to represent the member societies in Arab and International Women's conference and meetings.

6. To establish exhibitions and markets in the United Arab Emirates within the current laws and after obtaining the approval of the concerned authorities.

7. To publish and issue a periodic bulletin discussing research, studies and statistics relating to the women's activities in the United Arab Emirates.

8. To advise the Ministry of Social Affairs about every new women's society established in the United Arab Emirates.

The Women's Associations work across a number of areas such as education, heritage, health voluntary work, Girl Scouts and the development of skills and capabilities. In general, the associations make women's role visible in society, encouraging women to contribute, to develop and, indeed, to lead in the United Arab Emirates' continual growth. It is foreseen that the Women's Associations may provide a network for women in management to offer specific support for their efforts in the workplace.

## Favourable work-day design

One of the great benefits of working in Abu Dhabi is the shape of the working day: 7.00 a.m.–2.00 p.m. Saturday to Wednesday and 7.00 a.m.–12 noon on Thursday are the office hours in government, oil and banking organisations. Some private organisations work similar hours; others have a 'split shift' from 8.00/9.00 a.m. to 2.00 p.m. and from 4.00 p.m. to 7.00 p.m. Many work environments thus provide working parents with the opportunity to pick up children from school and to care for them during the afternoon and evening. Easy local commuting reinforces this practice. It is rare to travel more than 15 minutes to work. Housing is usually offered by the company and it is possible to live next door to the office, thereby eliminating all commuting. These practices compare favourably with the situation in the West, where one of the great barriers facing women in management is the constant conflict of demands between work and the family.

In a company culture survey conducted earlier this year with managers in the oil companies, the managers were asked to read through a deck of cards containing 17 value statements. They were told to discard the cards that did not reflect commonly held corporate values and then to rank the cards in their order of priority. The value card stating 'Commitments to family and life outside work are recognised' always appeared among the top five cards.

## Family-friendly culture of the United Arab Emirates

Hofstede's work on national and corporate cultures highlights some distinctive features of life in the United Arab Emirates. Hofstede was concerned with differences among national cultures at the consequences of these differences for the ways in which organisations are structured and managers behave. Using this framework he identified two dimensions in IBM:

1. *Individualism–Collectivism*. The tendency to take care of oneself and one's family versus the tendency to work together for the collective good of everyone.
2. *Masculinity–Femininity*. The extent to which highly assertive values predominate (e.g. acquiring money and goods at the expense of others) versus sharing sensitivity and concern for the welfare of others.

Hofstede included the United Arab Emirates as part of his Middle East sample and found that the Middle East countries that he did study rated in the middle of his Individualism scale, half-way between the high-rating of the United States, Australia and the United Kingdom on the one hand, and the low-rating Latin American dictatorships on the other. This finding demonstrates itself in everyday life in the United Arab Emirates, where there is a real sharing of family responsibilities. The family is the bedrock of Arab society and responsibility for the family does not lie solely with the mother as it does in western society. The UAE father plays an active role in the family. It is common for fathers to rush home promptly at 2 p.m. during the month of June to help children with their exams. Families out shopping in the modern shopping malls of Abu Dhabi are a frequent sight in the late afternoons and evenings. Fathers regularly take time off work to collect members of their family from airports or to take them to medical centres for treatment.

In a recent study of masculinity and British managers, Michael Roper[3] concluded that 'Masculinity is evident across a range of domains in management: as part of the collective discourses about business, as an aspect of particular business regimes, and most important . . . as a part of the self-image of male managers'.[3] According to Hofstede's results, the Arab countries rate as moderately masculine on the masculine–feminine index, whereas Japan, the United States and the United Kingdom rate highly on the masculine scale (see Figure 9.2 and Tables 9.1 and 9.2[4]).

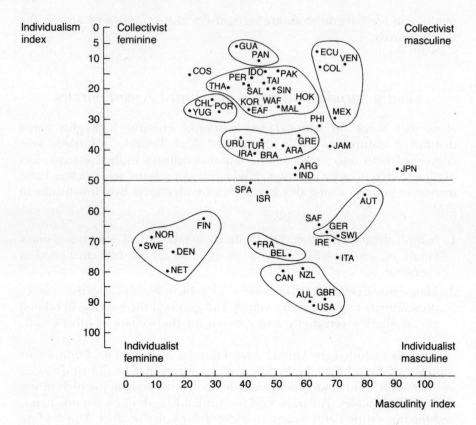

**Figure 9.2** The position of 50 countries and three regions on the masculinity–femininity and individualism–collectivism dimensions (for country name abbreviations see Table 9.1). *Source*: Hofstede, Geert H., *Cultures and Organizations, Software of the Mind*, McGraw-Hill International (UK) Limited, London 1991.

Achievement attributes are strongly emphasised in masculine societies and it is believed to be important to have an opportunity for advancement to higher level jobs and to have challenging work, from which one can achieve a personal sense of accomplishment. In feminine societies 'relationship attributes' are more important than achievement attributes; it is more important to have a good working relationship with one's direct superior, to work with people who cooperate well with one another, to live in an area desirable to oneself and one's family, and to have employment security so that one will be able to work for one's company as long as one chooses. It is interesting to note that the Arab countries rate almost equally highly on masculine and feminine characteristics, supporting the Arab commitment to their country, organisations, families and Islam.

**Table 9.1** Abbreviations for the countries and regions studied.

| Abbreviation | Country or region | Abbreviation | Country or region |
|---|---|---|---|
| ARA | Arab-speaking countries | ISR | Israel |
| | (Egypt, Iraq, Kuwait, | ITA | Italy |
| | Lebanon, Libya, Saudi | JAM | Jamaica |
| | Arabia, United Arab | JPN | Japan |
| | Emirates) | KOR | South Korea |
| ARG | Argentina | MAL | Malaysia |
| AUL | Australia | MEX | Mexico |
| AUT | Austria | NET | Netherlands |
| BEL | Belgium | NOR | Norway |
| BRA | Brazil | NZL | New Zealand |
| CAN | Canada | PAK | Pakistan |
| CHL | Chile | PAN | Panama |
| COL | Colombia | PER | Peru |
| COS | Costa Rica | PHI | Philippines |
| DEN | Denmark | POR | Portugal |
| EAF | East Africa (Ethiopia, | SAF | South Africa |
| | Kenya, Tanzania, | SAL | Salvador |
| | Zambia) | SIN | Singapore |
| ECU | Ecuador | SPA | Spain |
| FIN | Finland | SWE | Sweden |
| FRA | France | SWI | Switzerland |
| GBR | Great Britain | TAI | Taiwan |
| GER | Germany | THA | Thailand |
| GRE | Greece | TUR | Turkey |
| GUA | Guatemala | URU | Uruguay |
| HOK | Hong Kong | USA | United States |
| IDO | Indonesia | VEN | Venezuela |
| IND | India | WAF | West Africa (Ghana, |
| IRA | Iran | | Nigeria, Sierra Leone) |
| IRE | Ireland (Republic of) | YUG | Yugoslavia |

*Source*: Hofstede, Geert H., *Cultures and Organizations, Software of the Mind*, McGraw-Hill International (UK) Limited, London 1991.

## Support for child-care arrangements

One of the great barriers facing employed mothers in the West is the difficulty and expense of child-care. The infrastructure of society in the United Arab Emirates makes life much easier for the employed mother. The centrality of the family and the closeness of family relationships means that parents or parents-in-law often will help with the children. In the last generation women generally married young; hence they are often grandmothers in their thirties and forties, while they still have plenty of energy for child-care. In addition cheap domestic help is always available, due to the plentiful supply of Filipino and Indian women who come to the Middle East in desperate need of work. Employing organisations are

**Table 9.2** Cultures and organisations.

Masculinity index (MAX) values for 50 countries and 3 regions

| Score rank | Country or region | MAS score | Score rank | Country or region | MAS score |
|---|---|---|---|---|---|
| 1 | Japan | 95 | 28 | Singapore | 48 |
| 2 | Austria | 79 | 29 | Israel | 47 |
| 3 | Venezuela | 73 | 30/31 | Indonesia | 46 |
| 4/5 | Italy | 70 | 30/31 | West Africa | 46 |
| 4/5 | Switzerland | 70 | 32/33 | Turkey | 45 |
| 6 | Mexico | 69 | 32/33 | Taiwan | 45 |
| 7/8 | Ireland (Republic of) | 68 | 34 | Panama | 44 |
| 7/8 | Jamaica | 68 | 35/36 | Iran | 43 |
| 9/10 | Great Britain | 66 | 35/36 | France | 43 |
| 9/10 | Germany FR | 66 | 37/38 | Spain | 42 |
| 11/12 | Philippines | 64 | 37/38 | Peru | 42 |
| 11/12 | Colombia | 64 | 39 | East Africa | 41 |
| 13/14 | South Africa | 63 | 40 | Salvador | 40 |
| 13/14 | Ecuador | 63 | 41 | South Korea | 39 |
| 15 | USA | 62 | 42 | Uruguay | 38 |
| 16 | Australia | 61 | 43 | Guatemala | 37 |
| 17 | New Zealand | 58 | 44 | Thailand | 34 |
| 18/19 | Greece | 57 | 45 | Portugal | 31 |
| 18/19 | Hong Kong | 57 | 46 | Chile | 28 |
| 20/21 | Argentina | 56 | 47 | Finland | 26 |
| 20/21 | India | 56 | 48/49 | Yugoslavia | 21 |
| 22 | Belgium | 54 | 48/49 | Costa Rica | 21 |
| 23 | Arab countries | 53 | 50 | Denmark | 16 |
| 24 | Canada | 52 | 51 | Netherlands | 14 |
| 25/26 | Malaysia | 50 | 52 | Norway | 8 |
| 25/26 | Pakistan | 50 | 53 | Sweden | 5 |
| 27 | Brazil | 49 | | | |

*Source*: Hofstede, Geert H., *Cultures and Organizations, Software of the Mind*, McGraw-Hill International (UK) Limited, London 1991.

also supportive of the female manager's role in bringing up her children. Generous maternity leave is available (six months seemed to be the popular choice) and women who return to work while continuing to breastfeed are allowed an additional two hours off each day to return home to feed the baby. This practice is fostered by living close to one's employing organisation. The big organisations also provide family health clinics and their living compounds usually have grocery stores, parks, swimming pools, libraries and other facilities for children. Since the school day for children coincides with the working day of most big public sector organisations (7.00 a.m.–2 p.m.) it is possible for the working mother or father to balance work time and family time.

It is noteworthy that in all their working trips to the United Arab

Emirates the authors have never come across any expressed needs for a programme on 'managing stress'! In a country that thrives on the latest trends in training, it is fascinating that stress is not perceived to be a problem. Perhaps the ease with which Arab managers find sufficient time for family life is a contributor to a high-quality, balanced lifestyle. Perhaps a congruence between religious values and personal values also reinforces this lifestyle.

## Changing women's attitudes

Five women managers in a major Abu Dhabi oil company were interviewed in the summer of 1993, in order to obtain their views on the changing role of women in management in the United Arab Emirates. All of them had graduated from the nation's university at Al Ain. They held jobs in finance, public relations, personnel and computing.

The experience had lured them into further studying and into aspiring for a serious professional role in society. Each of the five women had felt frustrated about living at home after graduating. One woman, a 23-year-old human resource planner, tolerated it for six months because her father did not want her to work. However, she finally sent her CV to one company, was offered a post, and finally convinced her father to let her take the job. His two conditions were that she should cover her hair and that she did not share an office with any male colleagues. She has been with the company for two years now. She is ambitious, enthusiastic and prepared to work hard to succeed. She is attending an American university (South Eastern) to study management part time. Her day is a long one – from 7.00 a.m. to 2.00 p.m. at work and 4.00 p.m. to 10.00 p.m. at university. She drives her own car – another sign of recent female emancipation. When asked what she thought of the female dominance in graduate education in the United Arab Emirates she said: 'Women are prepared to work much harder. That's why they do so well at university.'

Talking about her future was like talking to any ambitious MBA graduate, 'I'd like to be Head of Personnel', she said. She is clearly excited about the career opportunities in front of her. Asked what she would do if she felt she was not progressing sufficiently, the answer was quick. 'I'd change companies!' She realises, of course, that women were expected to marry in the United Arab Emirates, hence her future husband would have to support her role as a career woman. Her mother or a housekeeper would help to look after her children.

An editor of an oil company in-house journal specifically looked for a job in an oil company that she perceived as being a modern organisation, well organised and democratic, and generally offering high rates of pay. She enjoys her work immensely. Her family has always supported her wish to work, as does her husband of four months. If and when she has children, she envisages her mother-in-law helping her. She feels that there is equality between men and women at her company and is positive about her future prospects. It is fascinating talking to these young women who represent the beginning of a new wave of managers in the United Arab Emirates. Despite their very protected upbringing they seem to be comfortable working in this macho, male-dominated oil industry.

Radical change has typified life in the United Arab Emirates, where families who lived in huts on the beaches or in desert communities have graduated to opulent accommodation and professional careers in prosperous companies in the big modern cities. Against this backdrop of unprecedented change over the past 40 years, the move to include women in management has attracted little public attention.

## The resisting forces for change

It would be wrong to underestimate the strength of the resisting forces to progress for women in management. These forces include negative male attitudes towards employed women, flawed human resource strategies among most UAE companies and a misunderstanding or misuse of Islamic belief.

### Negative male attitudes towards employed women

The UAE Arab husband often thinks the primary role of the woman to whom he is married is that of wife and mother, and he thinks that he should be the better educated of the two. Traditionally, Arab men often choose to marry a woman at around the age of 16, which precludes any tertiary education for her and establishes him as the sole breadwinner. Such attitudes are changing and we found that the younger, well-educated Arab men were often proud to be married to well-educated, ambitious women in management.

It is common practice in the United Arab Emirates for a married couple to visit both sets of in-laws during the week. Such a family custom gives a woman's parents a greater influence than they might have in the West. If they are overly protective towards their daughter they may have a negative attitude to her working when she is single, and this attitude may carry over, fuse with, and reinforce her husband's negative attitude towards her outside employment. Like the husband's attitude, the parents' attitude may cause them to see their daughter as preparing only for her life role as wife and mother, excluding work outside the home. Their attitude may even reflect older, more traditional values than those of their son-in-law, who may have studied in the West and developed more liberal attitudes to women in general and towards women managers in particular. Many Arab students marry western women while studying abroad and may face the issue of having a wife who wants to work in her professional or business field as she would in her home country, which can fly in the face of the negative attitudes towards female employment.

In 1993 President Sheikh Zayed, supported by the Women's Federation, took the initiative of creating a Marriage Fund designed to offer financial support to young UAE men to marry local women and, at the same time, to curb the previously prevalent practice of demanding extravagant dowries that were often beyond the reach of all but the wealthy. The dowry practice actually encouraged men to marry overseas brides and left local women unmarried.

Sometimes the negative attitude towards employed women derives from managers. The ease with which they collaborate and share the credit jointly for work achievements is in contrast to more competitive masculine management styles. Given the participative approach to management that is currently advocated in the West and given the tribal, consultative style of Arab managers, there should be a need for more women in management positions in the Arab world. This should be a welcome development.

However, the sheer lack of numbers of women entering the managerial ranks creates a catch-22 situation for the women – a situation (no access to senior managerial work) from which the victim (the woman) cannot extricate herself because the means of escape (obtaining a senior managerial position) are precluded by prior conditions (an unspoken policy of not employing women for senior management posts). Women in the United Arab Emirates will not exercise fully their potential as managers as long as the management culture tends to exclude them from all but the lower management positions. Male managers have no experience or little experience of working with women as professional equals and may therefore feel no need for them. They erect barriers, whether consciously or otherwise, to women's entry into the workforce and to their advancement once there. As Robert Schrank put it: 'When females threaten to move into positions of power, men are threatened twice: first that they will lose their authority over women, and second, that they will lose prestige and standing with the male, that is the important members of the tribe.'[5]

## Flawed human resource strategies

Apart from deep-seated attitudes against women's employment, perhaps the major resisting force is the fact that most companies have flawed human resource strategies with no policies for gender diversity, a failure to facilitate the advancement of women as role models, a neglect of mentoring and sponsoring, a shunning of most forms of affirmative action and a refusal to establish women-only management training, while engaging in tokenism.

## Omitting a policy on employee diversity

During the last seven years, since the publication in the United States of a study by the Hudson Institute called *Workforce 2000*,[6] the management literature has explored the concept of managing employee diversity as a scarce resource and for a competitive advantage. The policies for managing a diverse workforce, such as that created by the entry of women into a previously all-male world, are often linked to demographic changes in the workforce which will result in fewer male white workers by the year 2010.

Talented young people from the so-called rainbow (multicoloured) workforce will look to companies that have truly managed employee diversity as their preferred places of employment and career opportunity, giving these companies a competitive advantage. As global marketing increases, companies with rainbow workforces will have managers and other employees who really reflect the markets they serve, again gaining competitive edge.

## The absence of female role models

Female role models are important to women in management everywhere. As more women enter the ranks of senior management, these successful women serve as role models to their more junior colleagues. By their very presence in the company, operating at the highest levels, these female role models serve as an inspiration to others and as living proof that the glass ceiling can be shattered.

In the United Arab Emirates, at this time, there are very few female role models. Their absence deprives women who are on the first rungs of the managerial ladder from acquiring inspirational examples of women who have been successful. This serves as a resisting force for change.

## No policy of mentoring or sponsoring

Linked to the absence of female role models is the fact that even the most enlightened UAE companies do not have a policy of mentoring female managers. In the West the mentoring of women who aspire to more senior management positions is often an expressed company policy created in order to redress the sex balance or to facilitate the more aggressive approaches of affirmative action. By not expressly providing mentors for their female employers, UAE organisations are denied:

1. Easier recruitment and induction.

2. Improved motivation of both the protégé and the mentor.
3. A stable corporate culture in which the mentor passes on the corporate values to the protégé.
4. Improved communications, as mentoring cuts across functional departments and levels.
5. Savings in training and development costs, as compared to external courses and internal training programmes.
6. Rapid development of high fliers.
7. Organisational improvement resulting from targeted projects assignments.

A lack of mentoring means that the organisation loses the richness of management style provided by women managers. As Charles Handy observed:

> For these jobs the organisations want quality people, well educated, well skilled and adaptable. They also want people who can juggle with several tasks and assignments at one time, who are more interested in making things happen than in what title or office they hold, more concerned with power and influence than status. They want people who value instinct and intuition as well as analysis and rationality, who can be tough but also tender, focused but friendly, people who can cope with these necessary contradictions. They want, therefore, as many women as they can get.[7]

### Affirmative action

The American Civil Rights Law of 1963 began the era of affirmative action in which the United States government tried to force equal employment opportunities and to redress the racial imbalances of the past by positive discrimination in favour of blacks and by the quota system. Every government institution was required to have a certain percentage of black employees. Every outside contractor providing goods or services for the US government was required to follow clauses in government contracts that specified the racial mix of their workforce. The response to this forced change was often grudging compliance. Sometimes these government programmes were viewed as unnecessary and wasteful. In essence, the government's well-intentioned action too often reinforced the mistaken historical view that diverse people were not qualified and that affirmative action was a poor but necessary compromise.

Advocates of women's rights in America took up their struggle against sex discrimination in employment using the civil rights model and strategies. 'Affirmative action' and 'positive discrimination in favour of women' became part of their vocabulary and one of their demands. There is a 'Glass Ceiling Act' in the United States outlawing discrimination against women.

No one can doubt the concrete results of affirmative action in both the American Civil Rights struggle and in the American women's movement, but these are both historical experiences that are culturally and historically specific. In using the law one must always remember that one is using a blunt, heavy-handed instrument. If there are better ways of making the changes – for example, through voluntary efforts or by building a strong business case based on competitive advantage – one should promote these means.

### Tokenism

The danger of compulsory, legalistic programmes is that they easily lead to tokenism. No one who wants effective social change is happy with tokenism, especially not with being the token black in a law firm or the token woman in a senior position of a Gulf oil company. Special efforts, whether voluntary or compulsory, spontaneous or policy-driven have to be mounted to create the critical mass of women's involvement in order to make a difference, be it in the training room or the conference room.

Special single-sex management development programmes might be a preferred option. The case for women-only management education is a powerful one.

## Misunderstanding Islamic belief

There is nothing in the Qur'ān that supports unequal rights for women in employment or that forbids women to seek higher level jobs in management. Mrs Tansu Ciller, prime minister of the male-dominated Muslim country of Turkey, was elected to her position in June 1993 and is the third female leader of a Muslim nation, behind Pakistan's Benazir Bhutto and Bangladesh's Khaleda Zia. She is a successful, independently wealthy woman, a wife of 30 years and a mother with two sons aged 22 and 13. In June 1993 she proclaimed to a packed sports stadium in Ankara, Turkey's capital 'I am your mother, your soul sister!' and the crowd roared its approval.

Mrs Ciller's story is a demonstration of a life with a focus on education. From the age of 14, she wanted to be an economist. She used to discuss politics with her father, then the mayor of Istanbul. She was an only daughter and when, at the age of 17 in her last year of secondary school, she married fellow student Ozer Ucuran, he took *her* last name because she had no brothers to continue the family line. Marriage usually meant the end of education for a woman but she spent her honeymoon on a ship preparing for her university entrance exams, with her husband giving her extra calculus coaching. She did PhD work at the University of Connecticut and at Yale, but returned to Turkey in 1974 where, within nine years, she became the youngest full professor in her country. Later she became finance minister and head of her own party – the True Path Party – and then later, prime minister.

However, despite the fact that Mrs Ciller is a role model to the men and women of her country, there is a clear emphasis in Turkey on a woman's role as mother, which may be seen as a resisting force or may be used by those who resist change as a force to impede the emancipation of women. China's Mrs Rabia Kader, an ethnic Uighur Moslem who has built a business empire from nothing in Urumqui in the Xinjiang Province in the far west of China, made the point: 'Moslem women are normally supposed to stay at home and look after their husbands. It is very rare for a Moslem woman to travel so widely. A lot of people complained and were jealous.'[8] A mother of eleven children ranging in age from 3 to 30, this Muslim entrepreneur does not want to pass her 10 000-square-foot shopping centre on to her children. Instead she wants them to acquire knowledge and high technology. 'I will pay for their degrees in subjects which are useful to society because I did not have such an opportunity', she said.[8]

As a Muslim mother a woman is obliged to keep her child from any moral or physical harm, treat her child with compassion and love and provide the care needed for the child's growth and development. The Prophet Muhammad, reinforcing this exalted role of the mother in his Hadith (together with Sunna, traditional Muslim law), said:

> Someone asked the prophet, 'who deserves my service most after God?' The prophet said 'Your mother'. The person asked, 'And who is next?' The prophet replied 'Your mother'. The man asked for the third time, and the prophet said 'Your mother'. Then the man asked once more, 'And who is next?' and the prophet said 'Your father'.

From this teaching, religious Muslims conclude that three-quarters of a child's love and attention is due to the mother in Islam. In another Hadith the Prophet said '. . . paradise is under the feet of mothers'.

In the context of such a lofty role being allocated mothers, in a Muslim society it is understandable that a woman must balance carefully economic gain and career advancement with such serious and high expectations of herself as a mother. That is also the case for many women in the West, Muslim and otherwise, who have chosen to have families as well as managerial or professional careers.

Another part of the religious equation is the level of continuous appeal of the Prophet for all followers to seek perfection and to strive for a knowledge that is applicable to men and women alike. Qur'ānic verses and Hadiths can be cited to demonstrate this primacy of knowledge. 'Say: My Lord, increase my knowledge' (Holy Qur'ān xx: 1,14). 'God will exalt to high ranks those who believe among you, and those who have knowledge' (Holy Qur'ān LV111: 11). 'Seek knowledge from the cradle to the grave' (Hadith). 'The search for knowledge is a duty of every Muslim, male and female' (Hadith).

The roles of the Muslim woman, according to the Qur'ān and Sunna, are described as occupying three main roles – her role as a member of humankind, her role as a member of her family and her role as a member of society. None of these descriptions or prescriptions *per se* should hamper a woman's chosen career, although the intepretations that others place on the teachings may create some practical problems or a residue of attitudinal opposition to women assuming a more dramatic role in business or in corporate life, which becomes a resisting force for the change.

# Conclusion

In a recent review of women in management in the United Kingdom (1993),[9] Beverly Alimo-Metcalfe and Colleen Wedderburn-Tate conclude that the two biggest obstacles facing employed women are the lack of national strategies on child-care provision and on training. The United Arab Emirates provides a sharp contrast. The different national culture and infrastructure of society mean that child-care is not a significant issue in the United Arab Emirates. The massive government investments in education are reaping massive rewards, particularly for women.

It is early days for women in management in the United Arab Emirates. We cannot talk about 'glass ceilings' which are irrelevant in a country where women are just starting to infiltrate the lower levels of management. If women are to rise into senior levels, however, there will need to be significant changes in the attitudes of current senior male managers who are apt not to take women managers' careers seriously. The UAE government seems keen to promote women's active roles at work. In 1993 they published a book entitled *Women. The UAE Woman Progress*.[10] In it, Her Highness Sheikha Fatma Bint Mubarak says:

> The UAE gave women all their rights and never did it discriminate between both sexes whether in the right for an education or for scholarships abroad or for work opportunities and top executive posts. This is because Sheikh Zayed believes in women's ability to achieve progress.

> Some women have been promoted to senior jobs in the government in

the United Arab Emirates. It remains to be seen whether women make it to senior jobs in management across industry.

As Nancy A. Nicholls wrote:

> There seems to exist one universal approach: women of all ages and in all fields must continue to reach for the top in an unrelenting desire to fulfil themselves, to serve their employers and their families, and to create economic prosperity for themselves, their companies, and their countries. That, after all, is the only true measure of success.[11]

# References

1. *The United Arab Emirates*, Ministry of Information and Culture, Abu Dhabi, 1993.
2. *Annual Economic Report*, Ministry of Planning, *United Arab Emirates*, 1992.
3. Roper, Michael, *Masculinity and the British Organizational Man Since 1945*, Oxford University Press, Oxford, 1994.
4. Hofstede, Geert, *Cultures and Organizations, Software of the Mind*, McGraw-Hill, London 1991.
5. Schrank, Robert, 'Two women, three men on a raft', *Harvard Business Review*, May–June 1994, p. 78.
6. Johnson, William B. and Packer, Arnold H., *Workforce 2000*, Hudson Institute, Indianapolis, 1987.
7. Handy, Charles, *The Empty Raincoat, Making Sense of the Future*, Hutchinson, London, 1994, p. 179.
8. Nicoll, Alexander, 'Housewife who built empire from nothing', *Financial Times*, 9 June 1994, p. 6.
9. Alimo-Metcalfe, B. and Wedderburn-Tate, C., 'Women in business and management – the United Kingdom' in Cooper, C. L. and Davidson, M. J. (eds), *European Women in Business and Management*, Paul Chapman Publishing Ltd, London, 1993, pp. 16–43.
10. *Women. The UAE Woman Progress*, Ministry of Information and Culture, Abu Dhabi, 1993.
11. Nicholls, Nancy A. (ed.), *Reach for the Top, Women & The Changing Facts of Work Life*, The Harvard Business School Press, Boston, 1994.

# Author Index

143

# Subject Index